MEETING JESUS
in the Book of REVELATION

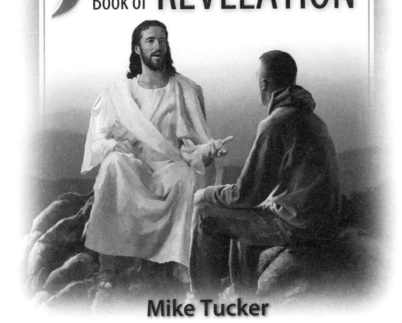

Mike Tucker

Pacific Press® Publishing Association
Nampa, Idaho
Oshawa, Ontario, Canada
www.pacificpress.com

Cover design by Gerald Lee Monks
Cover illustration by Lars Justinen
Inside design by Steve Lanto

Copyright © 2007 by
Pacific Press® Publishing Association
Printed in the United States of America

Additional copies of this book are available by calling toll-free
1-800-765-6955 or by visiting http://www.adventistbookcenter.com

Library of Congress Cataloging-in-Publication Data

Tucker, Mike (Michael Duane)
Meeting Jesus in the book of Revelation / Mike Tucker.
p. cm.
ISBN 13: 978-0-8163-2215-2
ISBN 10: 0-8163-2215-5
1. Bible. N.T. Revelation—Commentaries. I. Title.
BS2825.53.T83 2007
228'.077—dc22
2007017453

07 08 09 10 11 · 5 4 3 2 1

Other books by Mike Tucker

Heart Food

Jesus, He's All You'll Ever Need

Jesus, Your Heart's Desire

Journal of a Lonely God

Ten Keys to a Happy Marriage

A Time for You

Contents

Introduction 7

CHAPTER ONE   The One Who Loves You 13
               Revelation 1:1–7

CHAPTER TWO   The One Who Gives You Hope 24
               Revelation 1:8–18

CHAPTER THREE The One Who Meets Your Needs 31
               Revelation 2 & 3

CHAPTER FOUR   The One Who Is Worthy 43
               Revelation 4

CHAPTER FIVE   The One Who Ensures Victory 51
               Revelation 5

CHAPTER SIX   The One Who Controls All Things 58
               Revelation 6:1–8:1

CHAPTER SEVEN The One Who Dries Your Tears............... 69
               Revelation 7:9–17

CHAPTER EIGHT The One Who Defends You...................... 79
               Revelation 8:2–11:19

CHAPTER NINE   The One Who Planned Your Salvation..... 90
               Revelation 12 & 13

CHAPTER TEN   The One Who Rescues You.................... 102
               Revelation 14

CHAPTER ELEVEN   The One Who Forgives You 112
                 Revelation 14

CHAPTER TWELVE   The One Who Avenges You 122
                 Revelation 15–18

CHAPTER THIRTEEN The One Who Is Your Bridegroom 133
                 Revelation 19–21

CHAPTER FOURTEEN The One Who Prepares a Home for You... 145
                 Revelation 22

CHAPTER FIFTEEN The One Who Comes for You 151
                 Revelation 22

CHAPTER SIXTEEN The One Who Helps You Sleep at Night .. 158

Introduction

*A*lthough I grew up in a church that emphasizes the biblical book of Revelation, I've never liked it. In fact, when reading that book, or just hearing someone preach from it—I got nightmares.

My experience as a pastor tells me that I am not alone. Many others have had the same problem. A lot of good, church-going people wish the Bible had ended with Jude. Sixty-five books, instead of sixty-six, would have done quite nicely!

Many people have shared their stories with me—stories of fearful visions of strange science fiction–like beasts with bloodthirsty appetites. They are haunted by dreams of the end-time scenario painted by evangelists and the gut-wrenching, heart palpitating terror of being found unprepared for the final test. Nightmares of torture, hiding in the wilderness, and living like escaped convicts attempting to avoid capture—all interrupt their sleep. These people were terrorized by the knowledge that they had not memorized all of the proof texts and therefore could be subject to the deceptions of the end time.

Well-educated men and women have shared with me their unreasoning fear of the close of probation, the time of trouble, the seven last plagues, and of being lost. Thoughts of having one unconfessed sin paralyze them. They don't understand exactly what the dragon with seven heads and ten crowns, the beast from the sea, the beast from the land, and the whore of Babylon represent. These images are too weird, too frightening, and too disturbing for them to study. Their experiences of fear and uncertainty have caused them to hate the book of Revelation.

I can identify with their fears. They are telling my story, my experience with this book of the apocalypse.

When you are a pastor in a denomination that emphasizes Revelation, it is not a good idea to hate that book, so I decided to make a special study to see why this last book of the Bible seemed to carry such a startlingly different message than I had found in the sixty-five books that precede it.

What I found astonished me! The picture of Revelation that had been shared with me was inaccurate. I learned that any understanding of Scripture that creates an unreasonable fear is a false understanding, because Jesus Himself declared that He had not given us a "spirit of fear."

At the heart of this mysterious book of strange symbols and ominous forebodings is a portrait of Jesus. It is a picture so attractive as to make Him irresistible. I found messages of grace, hope, comfort, encouragement, and absolute assurance. I discovered Revelation assures us that the victory has already been won, and that we have absolutely nothing to fear as long as we cling to Jesus, our loving Savior!

So startling were my discoveries that Revelation has now become one of my favorite books of the Bible. Now I can actually read this great book and sleep peacefully at night.

I offer this devotional study of Revelation for one purpose: to help rid you of your fear of the end of time and the uncertainty that so many have experienced as they read the last book of the Bible. It is my hope that after reading my book, you will see in Revelation a masterpiece of God's great love.

Perhaps we will form a recovery group, sort of an AA for those who have lived in fear of Revelation. We will begin each meeting with, "Hello. I'm Mike, and I'm a Revelation-fear-aholic."

"Hi, Mike!"

"It's been thirty-four days since I last lost sleep over Revelation."

Applause!

Maybe that's not such a good idea. Instead, it might actually be better to join the group described in Revelation. This group does not share stories of fear or doubt. They simply sing a song that goes like this:

"Worthy is the Lamb, who was slain,
to receive power and wealth and wisdom and strength
and honor and glory and praise!" . . .
"To him who sits on the throne and to the Lamb
be praise and honor and glory and power,
for ever and ever!" (Revelation 5:12, 13).

After all, that is what this book is about. It is about Jesus, the Lamb of God, slain for your sins. It is about the victory He has won and His promise to share that great victory with you.

I invite you to take a look again at this marvelous book. As we look we will see a series of portraits of Jesus. Each portrait will reveal something different about the character and work of Jesus, the Hero of Revelation. One snapshot will show Him as the Source of our hope, another as our Deliverer, and yet another as our Defender. Each picture tells us something new about Jesus. Collectively, they place our hearts and our minds at ease.

During World War II, when the Nazis were bombing London, families sent their children to the country to live with families out of harm's way. As traumatic as this was on children and parents alike, it was far better than allowing the children to run the risk of serious injury or death.

Julie was a five-year-old who was sent to live with a family she had never met. It was a difficult time for this child. The family Julie stayed with was very nice, but they weren't *her* family.

One night Julie's host mother could hear the child's sobs, so she went in to comfort the child. After a few hugs and kind words, the woman made a suggestion. "Why don't you place the photograph of your mummy and daddy on the pillow next to you, and whenever you are frightened or feel lonely or homesick, you can turn the light on and look at your parents. If you imagine them being here with you it will make you feel better. You won't feel afraid anymore."

Julie found that it helped to look at Mummy and Daddy's photograph. It wasn't the same as having them right there by her side, but it helped. When Julie looked at the photograph, she remembered how much Mummy and Daddy loved her and how good it felt to be with them, and it helped.

Mummy and Daddy wrote letters often, and the nice lady Julie lived with would read the letters to her over and over again. Julie loved the words and would almost memorize each one, able to recite them by heart.

Finally the day came when Mummy and Daddy came to get Julie and take her home. It was a great day for Julie. Her parents gathered their little girl into their arms and hugged and kissed her and took her home to be with them.

That's what Revelation is. It is a series of photographs of the One who loves you and is coming to get you. He does not want you to be afraid, so He has given you photographs to remind you of how wonderful He looks to you. He has written letters to you to remind you of His love and to promise you that He is coming to get you and take you home. That's what Revelation is, a series of letters and photographs from the One who loves me and promises to come and take me home.

My hope is that my book will help you begin to think of Revelation differently than you have before. In the midst of this war-wracked planet, my prayer is that you will see the book of Revelation as a series of photographs and letters that will help you sleep peacefully rather than, as it has for so many, give you nightmares.

CHAPTER ONE

The One Who Loves You

Revelation 1:1–7

I've been exchanging e-mails with a student from a theological seminary in Egypt. He tells me that Jesus was a prophet but, definitely, not the Son of God. Though respecting Jesus, the seminarian tells me that Jesus did not die for our sins.

An overachieving, workaholic entrepreneur told me that Jesus has never held much of an appeal for him. Jesus seemed rather morose and preoccupied with His own death. "That sort of meek and mild disposition would," he said, "never make it in the dog-eat-dog business world I work in."

Who is Jesus? How do you think most people in the world would answer that question? How do most people see Jesus?

I am intrigued by the opening shots of the movie *La Dolce Vita*. This Italian movie opens with a shot of a helicopter and a giant statue of Jesus suspended underneath. The statue hangs in a sling with its arms outstretched as the helicopter approaches Rome.

People begin to recognize the statue. A farmer sees the helicopter, hops off his tractor, and races across the field shouting, "Hey, it's Jesus!" Girls sunbathing around a swimming pool look up and wave at the statue.

The expression on the statue's face seems sorrowful. He stares in silent disbelief at the modern world below.

Some people see Jesus as a lot like that hovering statue. Jesus looks down on a world He doesn't really understand. He is out of touch. He has no relevance in a world that has long ago passed Him by.

Who is Jesus, and how does He relate to us today? Ask that question of modern scholars and you get a confusing picture. Even biblical scholars disagree about Jesus. Some present Him as everything from a societal dropout to a militant revolutionary.

The best place to look for the answer to the question "Who is Jesus?" may not be with theologians. Sometimes the best answers to such questions are found in the mouths of babes.

Helen was three years old. One evening, Helen and her parents were dining at a Chinese restaurant. At the end of the meal her parents broke open their fortune cookies and read them aloud.

Helen wanted to "read" her fortune too. After breaking the cookie apart and retrieving the fortune, Helen announced proudly, "It says, 'Jesus loves me!' "

Who is Jesus? The simplest answer to this question may be the best. *Jesus is the One who loves you!*

Revelation is a book we do not usually think of as giving this picture of Jesus. I believe that when properly understood, however, Revelation paints a wonderful portrait of Jesus as *the One who loves us*.

Revelation is best understood as an unveiling of Jesus. The opening phrase of the book confirms this premise: "The revelation of Jesus Christ . . ." (Revelation 1:1).

This book was intended to reveal Jesus Christ to a world desperately in need of a glimpse of our Savior. It was intended to give us hope, to assure us of victory, and to put troubled minds at ease. John wants us to know that these words of comfort and hope are authentic. He received them from Jesus with a little help from an angel. "The revelation of Jesus Christ, which God gave him to show his servants what must soon take place. He made it known by sending his angel to his servant John, who testifies to everything he saw—that is, the word of God and the testimony of Jesus Christ" (Revelation 1:1, 2).

The book of Revelation reminds us that Jesus is sovereign, and that

He is ultimately victorious. It reassures us that those who can be counted among His followers will be victorious with Him.

There is another purpose for the book, the one most expositors focus on, which is to tell us the future. God wants us to know the things that will take place. However, even this purpose reveals Jesus and His character.

An ancient legend tells of a general whose army was afraid to fight. The enemy was too strong. Its fortress was too high and weapons too mighty. The general had an idea. He told his soldiers that he possessed a prophetic coin that would foretell the outcome of the battle. On one side was an eagle, on the other a bear. He would toss the coin. If it landed eagle-side up, they would win. If it landed with the bear side up, they would lose.

The army was silent as the coin flipped in the air. Soldiers circled as it fell to the ground. They held their breath as they looked and shouted when they saw the eagle. The army would win!

Bolstered by the assurance of victory, the men marched against the fortress and won. It was only after the victory that the king showed the men the coin. It had an eagle on both sides.

Though the story is fictional, the truth is reliable: *Assured victory empowers the army*. That may be the reason God gives us this revelation of Christ. In it He assures victory.

Christ knows that we face an awful battle. However, He does not want His children to be afraid. He loves us too much for that, so He tells us in advance exactly how the battle will end.

We, the soldiers, are privileged to have a glimpse into the final battlefield. At the end, all hell breaks loose as all heaven comes forth. The two worlds collide in the ultimate battle of good and evil. Left standing amidst the smoke and thunder is the Son of God.

Jesus, born in a manger, is now triumphant over Satan. Satan is defeated. Christ is triumphant. And we, the soldiers, are assured of victory.

Who is Jesus? He is the General who ensures victory. He assures you that there is no reason for fear, because He already knows how the battle will turn out! Jesus wins!

This revelation of Jesus was written to put your mind at ease. You are greatly loved! Your sins are forgiven! Your salvation is sure. The ultimate victory belongs to Jesus.

Revelation gives us wonderful portraits of our Savior, portraits that bring comfort to our fear-filled hearts.

George Macdonald wrote, "God hides nothing. His very work from the beginning is revelation—a casting aside of veil after veil, a showing unto men of truth after truth. On and on from fact divine he advances, until at length in his Son, Jesus, he unveils his very face."

This is what we find as we work through Revelation. We find that this mysterious book reveals wonderful photographs that become a source of comfort and hope.

In the first two verses of Revelation we find how this revelation of hope came to us. Verse 1 tells us that God gave it to Jesus, Jesus gave it to His angel, the angel took it to John, and John wrote the message down for us to read.

Revelation has been called the Apocalypse. *Apocalypse* simply means "unveiling." Through this book, God intends to pull back the curtain for us. That which was hidden will now be revealed.

What is God unveiling? Verse 1 tells us that God is revealing to us "what must soon take place." As the story of the army general and the prophetic coin would suggest, God wants us to know how the battle is going to turn out. We can peek at the final chapters of the book of the history of this world and find that Jesus wins—and we are told in some detail how all of this will take place.

Much of what John was to reveal about the future has already been fulfilled. Some is yet to come. But we are given a sneak peek at what lies ahead.

Revelation also unveils Jesus Himself. We are given a deeper look at the character of the Son of God, our Savior. In seeing a revelation of Jesus, we also see a revelation of God the Father, since, as Jesus told us, when we see the Son we also see the Father.

In this book, we find the loving concern of God for His children. We see God caring enough to show us that we do not need to be afraid.

Remember how the disciples reacted when Jesus told them He was going away from them? Jesus was speaking of His death, burial, and resurrection, but the disciples did not understand. Like young children whose parents are leaving on a trip, the disciples ask questions. "Where are You going? Can we come too? When will You come back?"

We tend to ask similar questions. "Jesus, where have You gone? Can we come there to be with You? When will You come to get us?" Revelation attempts to answer some of those questions. The Father is here attempting to put His children's minds at ease about the future. Yes, Jesus is away from us right now, but He is coming back soon. However, He doesn't want to lie to us, so He tells us that it may be a while and some difficult things will unfold in the meantime. But we don't have to worry, because our Father is bigger and stronger than any enemy we face, and eventually He will take us home with Him.

Verse 3 tells us that a blessing awaits us if we will read the letter and keep it. "Blessed is the one who reads the words of this prophecy, and blessed are those who hear it and take to heart what is written in it, because the time is near."

A blessing awaits all who read, hear, and keep this prophecy. A blessing awaits you. It has been my experience that the best blessings are the gift of Jesus Himself. When heaven desires to give the very best it can offer, it gives Jesus.

John,
To the seven churches in the province of Asia:
Grace and peace to you from him who is, and who was, and who is to come, and from the seven spirits before his throne, and from Jesus Christ, who is the faithful witness, the firstborn from the dead, and the ruler of the kings of the earth.

To him who loves us and has freed us from our sins by his blood, and has made us to be a kingdom and priests to serve his God and Father—to him be glory and power for ever and ever! Amen.

Look, he is coming with the clouds,
>   and every eye will see him,
>   even those who pierced him;
>   and all the peoples of the earth will mourn because of him.
>   So shall it be! Amen (Revelation 1:4–7).

John's opening greeting contains two gifts. Those gifts are grace and peace. Grace refers to all the gifts of the wondrous love of God that we cannot earn or deserve. R. C. Charles defines "peace" as "the harmony restored between God and man through Christ."

Already, God is putting our minds at ease by reminding us of the gifts we receive from His hand—grace and peace—undeserved gifts of love and a restored relationship with the Father.

But also notice the reference to the Trinity. First, we are given an interesting name for God the Father. "Him who is and who was and who is to come . . ." is a common reference to God the Father. It is a takeoff on the name God gave to Himself at the burning bush, "I AM that I AM" or "Yahweh."

The "seven Spirits who are before His throne" refers to the Holy Spirit. The number seven is the number of perfection and puts us in mind of the perfect and complete gifts of the Holy Spirit. The number seven in Hebrew means literally "Sabbath, cease, rest." Some of the churches in Asia to whom the letter was originally written were being persecuted. This was a promise that the Holy Spirit, who is the Creator of the church and Sustainer of the church, would use His gifts to provide a Sabbath rest even in the midst of persecution.

Finally, we have "Jesus Christ, who is the faithful witness." The message of Revelation comes from all Three Members of the Trinity. All of Them have joined Their immense talents together to paint a series of wonderful portraits of Jesus.

Verse 5 reminds those who could very well be martyred that Jesus has already won the victory over death. They have nothing to fear from the grave. "Jesus Christ, who is the faithful witness, the firstborn from the dead, and the ruler over the kings of the earth."

Jesus is the Giver of grace and peace. He is the Faithful Witness, the Firstborn of the dead.

There was a time during the most horrible persecutions of the Jews by the Nazis in Poland that an old Jewish cemetery keeper came into the cemetery one morning and found that during the night a woman had crept into an open grave and there given birth to a son. After she had given birth, she had died. The cemetery keeper found this child, and he said to everyone he saw, "This must be the Messiah, for only the Messiah could choose to be born in a grave."

Well, it wasn't the Messiah; the child died before noon of that day, but the cemetery keeper's conclusion spoke truth. Only the Messiah could choose to be born in a grave. Only a God who loves as our God loves could come into the midst of all the pain of our lives to bring His grace.

Jesus is the One who loves us, who has set us free from our sins by His blood. Jesus is the Ruler of kings on earth. He has made us a kingdom, priests, to His God and Father. To Him be glory and dominion forever!

Before John attempted to reveal to us the awesome and frightful things that were yet to come, He attempted to place the minds of his readers at ease. He did so by reminding them of perhaps the most important truth the world has ever known: Jesus is coming again.

It is as if John tells the readers: "Now, I'm going to say some frightening things, but do not be alarmed. Remember that you are the recipients of God's grace and peace. You are His special children, and He will care for you. Ultimately, Jesus will win the war, so don't allow the terrible battles to discourage you."

It does not matter what the future holds, because in the Trinity we have everything we need. God the Father is the One who ultimately is and was and is to come. He is this One who makes Himself known, the One who is the Author of grace and peace. The Holy Spirit is described as being in fellowship with the Father and Son and the One who from the presence of the Father and Son sends grace and peace to the churches. Jesus Christ is described in the most detail because He is the Living Word. In Jesus Christ, God is speaking for Himself, the very radical breakthrough of God in history.

Jesus Christ is God making Himself known as Lord, Savior, Victor over death, the One who loves and sets free by the event of His own suffering on our behalf, the One who is now our living Lord and who will come again. He will come, and all of His children will witness the event.

> Look, he is coming with the clouds,
>   and every eye will see him,
> even those who pierced him;
>   and all the peoples of the earth will mourn because of him.
>   So shall it be! Amen (Revelation 1:7).

Only a God of love would make such a promise!

Nothing makes sense without the return of Jesus. Without the Second Coming, there is no salvation, no hope, and no future. But for all who love Christ, His return is the most comforting promise in Scripture.

Jesus attempts to comfort the disciples with this thought in the fourteenth chapter of John: " 'Do not let your hearts be troubled. Trust in God; trust also in me. . . . And if I go and prepare a place for you, I will come back and take you to be with me that you also may be where I am' " (John 14:1, 3).

The book of Revelation provides a simple scenario: Jesus has gone away for a while, but He will return. Until then, He wants His children to be at peace. Isn't what Jesus promises wonderful? " 'Do not let your hearts be troubled. Trust in God; trust also in me' " (John 14:1).

Jesus doesn't want you to be anxious about things you cannot comprehend. If you don't understand the mark of the beast, the millennium, the judgment, and the seven last plagues, don't worry. Trust in Jesus; He will see you through.

If you are afraid that you will not be ready, trust in Jesus, and He will save you. "Do not let your hearts be troubled." Jesus is coming to get you so you can live with Him.

By the way, He has plenty of room for you. " 'In my Father's house are many rooms' " (verse 2).

Later in the book of Revelation, Jesus tells us the size of the city and reassures us that a place is prepared for us there. You will not be excluded—you will not be rejected. You are wanted in heaven.

All of heaven expects you and has made provision for you. Urban crowding is not a problem. " 'I am going there to prepare a place for you' " (verse 2). We will live in luxury with opportunities for both privacy and fellowship. Jesus has planned the city with you in mind. He has considered your needs, and your likes and dislikes.

A few years ago, a Kiwanis Club in Arlington, Texas, honored me as their "Man of the Year." A banquet was prepared, with me as the guest of honor.

As Gayle and I sat down to eat, a lovely plate was set before us. The main course at the banquet to honor me was pork chops. Gayle and I are Seventh-day Adventists, and members of our denomination do not eat pork!

Gayle and I ate around the meat. That fact did not go unnoticed. When asked, we explained that Seventh-day Adventists do not eat pork. They were terribly embarrassed! We tried to put their minds at ease by telling them that this was not a big deal, but their faces were red with embarrassment because they had not planned well for their guest of honor.

Rest assured that God has planned well for you. He has designed a place specifically for you. " 'I will come back and take you to be with me that you also may be where I am' " (verse 3).

Jesus is serious about coming for you. He is determined that your fearful mind be placed at ease. He will take care of you, and then He will return for you so you can be with Him forever.

George Tulloch displayed similar determination. In 1996 Tulloch led an expedition to the spot where the *Titanic* sank in 1912. He and his crew recovered numerous artifacts, everything from eyeglasses to jewelry to dishware.

Tulloch realized that a large piece of the hull had been broken from the ship and was resting not far from the vessel. Tulloch and his crew were thrilled by the prospect of recovering, not just a few artifacts, but a part of the ship itself.

The team began to lay plans to raise this rather large portion of the ship out of its watery grave and set it on their own boat. The portion of the *Titanic* they wanted to recover weighed about twenty tons.

Tulloch and his team actually lifted that huge chunk of iron to the surface, but a storm blew in and broke the ropes. The crew watched as the Atlantic reclaimed her treasure.

Time was running out, and the crew knew they would need to leave soon. But before Tulloch left, he did something curious. He descended once again to the floor of the ocean in his submarine, and with a robotic arm attached a strip of metal to a section of the hull. On the metal Tulloch had written, "I will come back, George Tulloch."

Why did George think it was necessary to leave a plaque? Did he think that someone would steal the *Titanic*? One would think that since the ship is two and one-half miles below the surface of the Atlantic, it would be safe. Besides that, it's a piece of junk. Who would want it?

Isn't this the same thing many have said about us? "What makes you think God would go to such lengths to rescue you? What possible value could you be to Him?"

Amazing as it may seem, when Jesus left the depths of this planet, He did something similar to what Tulloch did. He left a written promise of His return. "I will come back and take you to be with Me so that you may be where I am going."

Who is Jesus? Already we have learned something of Him. Jesus is the Revealer of secrets—the Revealer of those things yet to take place.

Jesus is also the Giver of the gifts of grace (undeserved forgiveness) and peace (a right relationship with God).

Jesus is the Faithful Witness. We can trust that everything He says is true and accurate.

As the Firstborn from the dead, Jesus is our assurance that death isn't the final answer to life. We will be resurrected from the grave, too, just as Jesus was.

We can trust that this is true because Jesus possesses all power. He is the true Ruler over the kings of the earth. We have nothing to fear of earthly governments. Jesus is the true Power behind all power. They can do nothing to you that He does not permit.

Jesus loves us and has provided for our salvation. He is our Savior, having shed His blood in a self-sacrificial act to set us free from the bondage of our sins. Jesus is the One who promises to give us positions of authority and honor. He will make us "kings and priests."

Jesus is the One who will return to take us to heaven so we will never experience the pain of separation again.

Jesus is our General who instills confidence in His followers by guaranteeing our ultimate victory. Assured victory empowers the army. Assured victory puts our minds at ease and gives us peace.

Jesus is the One who loves us.

This is the picture of Jesus given in the first seven verses of Revelation. In seven short verses, John the artist has painted with delicate detail the beginnings of a portrait of Jesus.

If this were all the information we had about Jesus, it would be enough for our salvation. We have learned much of our Savior, but we also learn something of who we are. We are beloved of God, priests on the earth, which means that we have a duty to minister to others. We are those who have been set free—set free from our sins and set free from the need to panic about the toils of our troubled generation. And finally, we are those for whom Christ is returning.

Who is Jesus?

Revelation tells us that He is the God who loves you, who redeemed you, and who is returning for you. Jesus is the God who assures you of victory in your life—victory today and victory as we face an uncertain future.

CHAPTER TWO

The One Who Gives You Hope

Revelation 1:8–18

I love the story of the high school basketball coach who was attempting to motivate his players to persevere through a difficult season. Halfway through the season, he stood before his team and said, "Did Michael Jordan ever quit?"

The team responded, "No!"

He yelled, "What about the Wright brothers? Did they ever give up?"

The team resounded, "No!"

"Did Walter Payton ever quit?"

Again the team yelled, "No!"

"Did Elmer McAllister ever quit?"

There was a long silence. Finally one player was bold enough to ask, "Who's Elmer McAllister? We've never heard of him."

The coach snapped back, "Of course you never heard of him—he quit!"

Revelation encourages us to never give up—to never quit.

In a far country lived a band of traveling minstrels who had not been doing well. Times were hard, and though their fees were small, there was little money for common folk to pay in order to come and hear them. Attendance had been falling off, so early one evening the group met to discuss their plight.

"I see no reason for opening tonight," one said. "To make things even worse, it is starting to snow. Who will venture out on a night like this?"

Another singer said, "I agree. Last night we performed for just a handful. Fewer will come tonight. Why not give back their meager fees and cancel the concert? No one can expect us to go on when just a few are in the audience."

A third singer asked, "How can anyone do his best for so few?"

Then he turned to another sitting beside him. "What do you think?"

This man was older than the three who had already spoken. He looked straight at his troupe.

"I know you are discouraged. I am too. But we have a responsibility to those who might come. We will go on. And we will do the best job of which we are capable. It is not the fault of those who come that others do not. They should not be punished with less than the best we can give."

Heartened by his words, the minstrels went ahead with their show. They never performed better.

When the show was over and the small audience gone, the old man called his troupe to him. In his hand was a note, handed to him by one of the audience just before the doors closed behind him.

"Listen to this, my friends!"

Something electrifying in his tone of voice made them turn to him in anticipation. Slowly the old man read, "Thank you for a beautiful performance."

It was signed very simply—"Your King."

Jesus knew that there would be days when it would be difficult for us to go on—days when we would want to quit. He knew there would be times of discouragement, loss, persecution, and difficulty.

So Jesus provided for such times of discouragement. He tells us that He understands how difficult it is to continue in adversity. But like a parent attending the ballgame of his child, Jesus cheers us on. He promises rewards for endurance. He promises help in difficult times. He reminds us that everything we do is done for an audience of One—and that audience is Jesus, our King. " 'I am the Alpha and the Omega,' says the Lord God, 'who is, and who was, and who is to come, the Almighty' " (Revelation 1:8).

Revelation was not written primarily to tell us about the future. It was written to tell us about the One who holds the future. This book is a revelation of our Lord, Jesus Christ.

The book promises us that we will be victorious. A promise is only as good as the one who makes the promise. John wants us to know that we have good reason to trust that the promise will be fulfilled.

Victory is assured because our God is the King of kings and the Lord of lords. He has always existed and always will exist. Before anything else existed, He was. He is the First and the Last, the Beginning and the End, and everything else in between. Our Sovereign God can assure us of victory because He has no rivals. God can do as He pleases, and it pleases Him that His children should be victorious.

Everyone who aligns himself with God will win. Everyone who chooses to worship the true God will gain the victory. God guarantees it!

John, the brother of James, wrote the book of Revelation. John had been arrested and sent to prison on Patmos, a rocky crag of an island in the middle of the Aegean Sea, some fifty miles southwest of the coast of Asia Minor. Today it is called Patina. In John's day it was used as a penal settlement. Visions came to John on this island, so John wrote them down and sent them to his fellow Christians. "I, John, your brother and companion in the suffering and kingdom and patient endurance that are ours in Jesus, was on the island of Patmos because of the word of God and the testimony of Jesus. On the Lord's Day I was in the Spirit, and I heard behind me a loud voice like a trumpet, which said: 'Write on a scroll what you see and send it to the seven churches: to Ephesus, Smyrna, Pergamum, Thyatira, Sardis, Philadelphia and Laodicea' " (Revelation 1:9–11).

When John says that he was in vision "on the Lord's Day," two different ideas come to mind. First, he could mean that he was in vision on Saturday, the Sabbath. The Sabbath is the only day that Scripture ever speaks of as belonging to God. No place in the New Testament is any other day referred to as enjoying the special blessing of God. This could mean that John had his vision on the Sabbath, the seventh day of the week.

Some scholars believe that John may have used the phrase "the Lord's Day" with reference to the eschatological day of the Lord. This could mean that John was saying that he was taken in vision in order that he might look forward to the coming of Christ. His visions would deal with the events leading up to the return of Jesus in the clouds of glory, thus the designation, "the Lord's Day."

Either way, what's most important is what the vision is saying to us.

The vision found in chapters 1–3 was primarily given for seven churches in Asia Minor. Although there would be some things in the vision that would be fairly difficult for some of these people to hear, ultimately the messages were all messages of hope and of encouragement to press forward to the ultimate victory.

I turned around to see the voice that was speaking to me. And when I turned I saw seven golden lampstands, and among the lampstands was someone "like a son of man," dressed in a robe reaching down to his feet and with a golden sash around his chest. His head and hair were white like wool, as white as snow, and his eyes were like blazing fire. His feet were like bronze glowing in a furnace, and his voice was like the sound of rushing waters. In his right hand he held seven stars, and out of his mouth came a sharp double-edged sword. His face was like the sun shining in all its brilliance (Revelation 1:12–16).

John, in vision, turned to see who was talking to him. When he did he saw "someone 'like a son of man.' " This is a phrase borrowed ultimately from Daniel. It is a Messianic title that Daniel used and that Jesus applied to Himself. In fact, while on earth, "Son of Man" was Jesus' favorite title for Himself. By this phrase, Jesus identified Himself as the promised Messiah, the Son of God, Savior of the world. It is with this title that Jesus is identified in verse 13.

He was walking among the seven golden lampstands, which represent the seven churches that Jesus addressed through these messages. That the churches are each represented by a lamp signifies the perfect, complete work of the Holy Spirit with each church. Each church had everything they needed provided by the Holy Spirit. He would support them in each task assigned to them.

Jesus is described as wearing a robe with a golden sash. His hair is white, His voice is as loud and clear as the sound of a great body of water, His eyes were burning, and His feet were solid, bright, and as strong as bronze. He holds in His hand the seven stars representing the leaders of the seven churches.

These are symbols of victory. This is a picture of the glorified Christ walking among the seven churches with their leaders in His hand. This fulfilled the promise of God that was given to ancient Israel. In Leviticus 26:11, 12, God promised that He would make His dwelling place with Israel. He would be their God and they would be His people.

Jesus has given each of us the full measure of His Holy Spirit. We have everything we need to complete the work assigned to us. Jesus Himself dwells within each of us. He is our God, and His presence assures us of victory. "When I saw him, I fell at his feet as though dead. Then he placed his right hand on me and said: 'Do not be afraid. I am the First and the Last. I am the Living One; I was dead, and behold I am alive for ever and ever! And I hold the keys of death and Hades' " (Revelation 1:17, 18).

When John saw this vision of the dignified, victorious, glorified Christ, it struck fear in his heart. We cannot look upon a Holy God without experiencing fear. We see the glory and the holiness of God. This draws a distinct contrast to us and to our sinful condition.

John saw all of this and became afraid. He collapsed to the ground, scarcely breathing. His heart was pounding as John experienced what the prophet Isaiah experienced in vision as he stood in the presence of a Holy God. Isaiah chapter 6 tells us that he too, fell to the ground as a dead man. His sinfulness made him fear for his very existence as he looked upon a God without sin.

Jesus spoke to John in order that He might reassure him. Literally, Jesus said, "Stop being afraid." Then Jesus told John why he should stop fearing. It was because Jesus is "the First and the Last." Like a parent holding a child's hand when the lights go out during a storm, Jesus takes your hand and whispers in your ear, "Don't be afraid. I'm here with you. I'll protect you."

As comforting as it is for a child to hear those words from a parent, it is far better to hear them from Jesus, for Jesus is God. He has the power to protect you. More importantly, He has the power to see you through to your home in heaven. He has that power by virtue of the fact that He is God.

The designation, "the First and the Last," meant that there was no god other than Jesus. By this designation, Jesus identified Himself as Yahweh, the name for God in the Old Testament. Jesus' very name is designed to take away fear.

Not only is Jesus God, but He is also the One who won the victory over death and the grave, an important point because those churches were going through persecution and even martyrdom. Jesus too had given His life, and yet He lives today. His victory over death reassures believers that He will give them the courage they need to remain faithful to death, and the assurance that they will live again because Jesus has overcome death and the grave.

Jesus is giving away the end of the book before we read it. He does this to take away our fear.

When I was a kid I enjoyed watching action movies. I use the word *enjoyed* rather loosely. The movies scared me to death. The hero's life hung in the balance. There appeared to be no way out. It seemed as though he would come to an untimely end. Finally, right at the end, the hero miraculously finds a way out, his life is spared, and truth and justice win.

When it appeared that the villains would win, I could hardly bear to watch. My mom would remind me, "It's going to be OK. I've seen this before. He gets out of this alive."

That's what Jesus is doing in the first chapter of Revelation. He's whispering in our ear, "I know it looks pretty frightening just now, but I've seen the end and I know who wins. I win and you win too, since you are on My side. Trust Me! It's going to be OK!"

We can live without fear because we know the identity of our Leader, Jesus Christ. He is King of kings, and Lord of lords. He is described as "someone like 'a son of man' dressed in a robe reaching down to his feet and with a golden sash around his chest. His head and hair were white like wool, as white as snow, and his eyes were like blazing fire. His feet were like bronze glowing in a furnace, and his voice was like the sound of rushing waters. In his right hand he held seven stars, and out of his mouth came a sharp double-edged sword. His face was like the sun shining in all its brilliance" (Revelation 1:13–16).

This is why we need not fear when we read Revelation. We know how the story ends. It ends with complete victory by our Leader. Jesus wins; God has the last word. As His followers, we experience His victory, and thus eternity is ours!

Chapter Three

The One Who Meets Your Needs

Revelation 2 & 3

I visited Larry in the hospital. Larry contacted me when he learned he was suffering with a potentially fatal disease. Needless to say, Larry was worried. Panicked, in fact.

Larry didn't want to die. He had a family to support. Larry worried whether or not they would be able to survive without him.

As concerned as Larry was about his family, he had an even deeper fear. Larry had drifted away from God and was certain that he was not fit for heaven.

It wasn't just that Larry didn't want to miss out on eternity. Larry wanted to be healed but felt very embarrassed about coming to God after all these years away from Him. How could he approach God now? Why would God listen to his prayer now, after Larry had ignored God for so long?

Larry's dilemma is not unique. Others feel uncertain about approaching God because they know their life is not what it should be. Larry believed that God doesn't waste His time on those who haven't measured up to some higher standard.

Larry's fears revealed a great misunderstanding. Larry and countless others believe that God is unwilling to do for them that which He does for those whom they suppose measure up to God's requirements.

Have you ever had similar thoughts about God? Have you ever been reticent to approach God with a request because you knew your life simply didn't measure up?

The purpose of Revelation is to reveal to us the truth about God as seen in Jesus. Jesus Himself told us that if we have seen Him we have, in fact, seen the Father, so as we look at Jesus' character, we see God's.

Revelation, a book that has been shrouded in mystery and used to strike fear into the hearts of readers, was intended to show us the character of God as revealed in Jesus.

However, the character of God is not revealed to us just in order that we might be better informed about God. Eugene Peterson writes, "The intent of revelation is not to inform us about God, but to involve us with God."

As we continue our study of this book of hope, the next thing we learn is this: Regardless of where you are in your spiritual life, God loves you and accepts you, and offers a promise to meet your most pressing need today.

Chapters 2 and 3 of Revelation contain messages given to seven churches in Asia Minor, messages given to John by Jesus Himself. The messages to the seven churches follow a fairly stable pattern. They include praise, criticism, a warning, exhortation, and a promise.

While there are many applications of this section of Revelation, I believe the most practical for us today is the idea that each of the seven churches represents different spiritual conditions of believers. Some of the churches represent those who are close to God, while others represent those who have drifted and are distant or openly rebellious. Yet Jesus speaks of all as though they are His special children. He loves and accepts all of them as they are and offers promises to meet their specific needs.

While Jesus encourages each church to experience growth in Him, He makes it clear that whether they are near to Him or far from Him, each is the object of His loving acceptance. Jesus claims each of the churches just as they are, and Jesus claims you just as you are right now.

Let's look at the message given to the church in the ancient city of Ephesus. " 'To the angel of the church in Ephesus write: These are the words of him who holds the seven stars in his right hand and walks among the seven golden lampstands: I know your deeds, your hard work and your perseverance. I know that you cannot tolerate wicked men, that you have tested those who claim to be apostles but are not, and have found them false. You have persevered and have endured hardships for my name, and have not grown weary' " (Revelation 2:1–3).

Ephesus was a wealthy city where trade and commerce prospered. The major trade routes of the region all went through Ephesus. From the city's port, one of the greatest seaports of the ancient world, goods flowed to every corner of the earth.

Ephesus was the home of the Panionian games. These annual athletic events saw athletes and fans pour into the city from the entire region.

The Temple of Diana, one of the seven wonders of the ancient world, was located in Ephesus. New Testament commentator William Barclay wrote that the Temple of Diana was an asylum for anyone who had committed a crime. This safety zone for criminals extended some two hundred yards from the Temple of Diana. Because of this, criminals from miles around were drawn to Ephesus. Ephesus didn't just tolerate lawbreakers; it embraced and protected them!

The entire city was notorious for immorality. Ephesus was thought of as a city full of criminals. It was in this environment that the members of the church at Ephesus attempted to live a Christian life.

The Ephesian church decided that they would live life by different standards. They would refuse to participate in the immoral practices that were accepted as the norm. They also held to true doctrine. They developed a special ability to spot false doctrine and refused to tolerate it.

Jesus has a special commendation for these people. He praised them for their ability to work hard. The members of the church in Ephesus had been able to grit their teeth, rebuke that which was wrong, and endure hard times. However, this was not a perfect church. " 'Yet I hold this against you: You have forsaken your first love' " (Revelation 2:4).

No doubt, the people in Ephesus were good people. They endured hardships and resisted false doctrine. But they were a lot like the man who Mark Twain described as being "a good man in the worst sense of the word." They did what was right, but for the wrong reasons.

We've all seen Christians who would never dream of intentionally committing a wrong act but seem to be so focused on avoiding evil that they never smile. This church was so intent on doing right that they had lost their first love for Jesus and, therefore, their love for each other. Their doctrine was pure, but they had lost their joy.

For everyone who finds himself in the spiritual condition of Ephesus, Jesus has a promise: " 'He who has an ear, let him hear what the Spirit says to the churches. To him who overcomes, I will give the right to eat from the tree of life, which is in the paradise of God' " (Revelation 2:7).

Jesus cures spiritual joylessness with a carrot rather than a stick. He promises that if you return to your first love for Jesus and allow that first love to give you a love for your fellow man and a joy for life, Jesus will give you paradise.

Notice, paradise comes as a result of pure love, not just pure doctrine and high standards of behavior. Jesus promises to return to you your first love for Him, and the resulting love for others.

Next comes the church at Smyrna, the modern day city of Izmir, Turkey. Smyrna was a church that had been slandered and persecuted but would endure even greater persecution later.

It was during this time of persecution that Polycarp was burned to death. Polycarp was a beloved Christian leader who was martyred when he was in his eighties. Some Jews in Smyrna were so anxious to be rid of Polycarp that they gathered firewood for his execution on the Sabbath. They were willing to break the Sabbath in order that they might execute this elderly Christian.

Jesus encouraged this church by reminding them that even the Son of God had been put to death: " 'To the angel of the church in Smyrna write: These are the words of him who is the First and the Last, who died and came to life again. I know your afflictions and your poverty—yet you are rich! I know the slander of those who say they are Jews and are not, but are a synagogue of Satan' " (Revelation 2:8, 9).

The church at Smyrna was poor in material goods and lived every day at great risk of persecution. Yet, as is often the case with persecuted people, they were rich in faith and love.

Because this was a persecuted church, Jesus gave no rebuke. Why would you rebuke people who are being martyred? Jesus only gave a promise that would help them endure: " 'Do not be afraid of what you are about to suffer. I tell you, the devil will put some of you in prison to test you, and you will suffer persecution for ten days. Be faithful, even to the point of death, and I will give you the crown of life. He who has an ear, let him hear what the Spirit says to the churches. He who overcomes will not be hurt at all by the second death' " (Revelation 2:10, 11).

Jesus identifies with this persecuted church by reminding them that He was persecuted as well, and by promising them that although they may suffer martyrdom, their reward would be eternal life.

The organization Voice of the Martyrs estimates that more Christians are being persecuted for their faith today than at almost any other time in history. Most of us tend to think of persecution and martyrdom as something from the past, the Middle Ages and so forth. Yet many Christians are persecuted today and even martyred in communist countries and in countries with a strong Islamic government. In those countries, people who attempt to evangelize or those who convert from Islam to Christianity do so often at great peril.

Persecution is not limited to communist and Islamic countries. While governments in free, democratic countries are not persecuting Christians, persecution still occurs. I have seen families disown a son or daughter who converted to Christianity. Friends often bring great pressure to bear against a colleague who takes a stand for Christ. Some are ostracized for their newfound faith.

If you are being persecuted for your faith, hold on to your love for Jesus! Be faithful to Him, and He will be with you always, and He will give you eternal life!

Next, Jesus addresses the church in Pergamum. Pergamum was a capital city for the Roman province of Asia. It was a center of culture and education, boasting a library that contained two hundred thousand scrolls, making it the second largest library in the ancient world.

But Pergamum was also home to temples to several pagan gods, including a temple to the Emperor Augustus. It was also the first city to embrace emperor worship. Emperor worship was compulsory in Pergamum, being required in order to conduct business—to buy and to sell.

Once a year citizens had to go to the emperor's temple, offer incense to a statue of the emperor, and proclaim, "Caesar is lord!" When this was done, a certificate was issued that permitted you to conduct business. Those who failed to do this were persecuted.

Jesus said of Pergamum: " 'I know where you live—where Satan has his throne. Yet you remain true to my name. You did not renounce your faith in me, even in the days of Antipas, my faithful witness, who was put to death in your city—where Satan lives' " (Revelation 2:13).

Jesus said that He understood the difficulties the Christians in Pergamum faced. Satan was active in that city, and his activity was causing trouble for Christians.

But not all of the Christians in that city had remained faithful. Some were even teaching that it was a good idea to make a small compromise on emperor worship in order to avoid persecution. Jesus declared that it was always a mistake to compromise principle for the sake of expediency. Jesus urged Pergamum to remain faithful and He made two promises to them. " 'He who has an ear, let him hear what the Spirit says to the churches. To him who overcomes, I will give some of the hidden manna. I will also give him a white stone with a new name written on it, known only to him who receives it' " (Revelation 2:17).

If you have compromised for the sake of expediency, Jesus urges you to remain faithful and promises that a new name will be given to you, one written in stone, which suggests that your good name will be restored. He also promises that you will dine in heaven with Him, eating manna, the bread of the angels.

Whether you have lost your first love, or are persecuted for your faith, or have compromised in order to avoid persecution, Jesus loves and accepts you and has a promise for your need today.

Now we turn to the church in Thyatira. There was much that was good with this church, as is indicated by verses 18 and 19, where the members are praised for their good deeds, their love and faith, and their increasing perseverance. However, this was a church with a significant sin problem. " 'Nevertheless, I have this against you: You tolerate that woman Jezebel, who calls herself a prophetess. By her teaching she misleads my servants into sexual immorality and the eating of food sacrificed to idols' " (Revelation 2:20).

Thyatira was a small, insignificant city whose citizens were not prosperous. The citizenry was primarily laborers and tradesmen. Thyatira had a great many trade guilds. In order to have a job, a worker must belong to a trade guild. Guild members were expected to participate in pagan festivals, which included eating meat offered to an idol, drunkenness, and engaging in sexually immoral activities, often with temple prostitutes.

One female member of the church in Thyatira claimed to be a prophet and taught that Christians should go along with the requirements for entrance to the trade guilds in order that they might be employed and earn money. Many had listened to her and were also conforming to the deviant sexual practices of that culture.

How is this unlike today? I find few who have entered into sexual sin for the purposes of employment, but I have found many who have made compromises with the sexual mores of this day. They have attempted to explain away their behavior by attacking, as outdated, the biblical standard of sexual purity.

The Bible clearly teaches abstinence before marriage and fidelity in marriage. When this standard is compromised, disaster results.

I cannot tell you how many times I have listened as someone, with great anguish, spoke to me about some sexual sin. Sexual sin can leave a person feeling unlovable and unacceptable to God in ways other types of sin cannot.

But God has a message to those who have fallen into this type of sin. Jesus says:

> To him who overcomes and does my will to the end, I will give authority over the nations—
> "He will rule them with an iron scepter;
>   he will dash them to pieces like pottery"—
> just as I have received authority from my Father. I will also give him the morning star (Revelation 2:26–28).

Far from being an outcast, those who repent of sexual sin and remain faithful will become leaders and rulers. Jesus promises to give them "the morning star."

Jesus is the Morning Star! Jesus promises to give those who are recovering from sexual immorality the gift of Himself—a gift that cannot be taken from you. You may feel separated from Jesus because of your sin, but Jesus promises to heal any separation with the gift of His eternal presence.

If the four spiritual conditions we have mentioned in chapter 2 do not apply to you, perhaps you can resonate with the first spiritual condition mentioned in chapter 3.

Were you once close to the Lord, but now have fallen into a spiritual funk? Do you find yourself dying a slow, agonizing, spiritual death? Have you lost interest in spiritual things, slipping into a sort of spiritual lethargy? If so, the message to the church at Sardis is for you.

Sardis was, at one time, a prosperous and glorious city. By the time of the writing of the book of Revelation, the glory days for Sardis were over.

The city was built at the top of a hill with such a steep slope as to make it very difficult for invading armies to capture the city. City officials placed far too much trust in this natural barrier to invasion and often chose not to post a guard on the city walls. On two separate occasions, an invading army captured Sardis almost without a fight. The soldiers climbed the hill at night, found no guard on the walls, and took the city easily.

The citizens of Sardis clung to past glories, refusing to accept the city's vulnerability, and therefore failed to keep watch. Jesus had the following message to Sardis: " 'To the angel of the church in Sardis write: These are the words of him who holds the seven spirits of God and the seven stars. I know your deeds; you have a reputation of being alive, but you are dead. Wake up! Strengthen what remains and is about to die, for I have not found your deeds complete in the sight of my God' " (Revelation 3:1, 2).

Perhaps you have heard people talk about how great it was in years gone by. They remember how alive the church was, and how they were aglow with the glory of God!

Those who speak this way often do so because they have nothing happening today to share. Their glory is past, and their future is as uninspiring as their lackluster spiritual life is today! Their spirituality is half-hearted, their devotion divided.

Jesus urges these Christians to awaken from their spiritual slumber, and He promises that if they will wake up and keep watch, their glory will never fade.

" 'Yet you have a few people in Sardis who have not soiled their clothes. They will walk with me, dressed in white, for they are worthy. He who overcomes will, like them, be dressed in white. I will never blot out his name from the book of life, but will acknowledge his name before my Father and his angels' " (Revelation 3:4, 5).

Wake up! Keep watching, and Jesus will make your salvation sure!

If fading glory and spiritual lethargy do not describe your spiritual condition, you may be able to identify with the church of brotherly love, Philadelphia. Philadelphia was founded to be a center for spreading the Greek culture and language. It was described as an "open door" to the world.

Philadelphia was also well suited to be a center for the spreading of Christianity, largely because the members of this church understood the essence of Christianity. This group of people held fast to Jesus. They had been slandered, but still, they held on. The believers in Philadelphia loved each other and demonstrated their love through their deeds.

No criticism is given for this church, only encouragement. Certainly, these people were not perfect, but they attempted to live out the principles of the gospel through their love for each other and their faithfulness to Jesus. They were obedient to Jesus and held to pure doctrines. To this group of faithful, loving, and gracious people, Jesus promised, " 'I am coming soon. Hold on to what you have, so that no one will take your crown. Him who overcomes I will make a pillar in the temple of my God. Never again will he leave it. I will write on him the name of my God and the name of the city of my God, the new Jerusalem, which is coming down out of heaven from my God; and I will also write on him my new name' " (Revelation 3:11, 12).

If you are one who, by God's grace, has kept your first love of Jesus and have attempted to share that love with those around you, Jesus promises to come for you. He has promised to make you a permanent fixture in heaven, and to never leave you. Jesus promises you eternity, not because you are perfect but because you trust in His perfection and have allowed His love to change your life.

There is one last church. Laodicea was located at a crossroads and was a center of trade. The city was enormously wealthy and proud of its wealth. Most of their money came from the clothing industry and from banking transactions. They exported soft, black, woolen garments and wool carpets all over the world. The banks of the city stored vast quantities of gold.

This church represents those lukewarm Christians—those who feel self-sufficient and satisfied with the status quo. Jesus says to this church: " 'I know your deeds, that you are neither cold nor hot. I wish you were either one or the other! So, because you are lukewarm—neither hot nor cold—I am about to spit you out of my mouth. You say, "I am rich; I have acquired wealth and do not need a thing." But you do not realize that you are wretched, pitiful, poor, blind and naked' " (Revelation 3:15–17).

Members of the church in Laodicea were good people. They were people you would describe as "the salt of the earth." They were honest and hard-working. However, they were proud of their personal virtues and believed that they could solve any problem through industry and through their wealth. This pride, however, prevented them from seeing their spiritual poverty.

These people were not cold to God, but they weren't on fire either. It was a lukewarm church. The church believed it had everything it needed.

Jesus, during His earthly ministry, spoke of the spiritual blindness of the Pharisees and priests, who were puffed up with pride at their own good works, thinking that they were good enough for heaven based on the good things they did and the bad things they avoided. They were careful to keep the Sabbath by observing meticulously a long list of Sabbath laws. They paid their tithes and offerings carefully, but they were cold, unloving, and harshly condemnatory toward their spiritual "inferiors."

When the Pharisees compared themselves with others, they felt pretty good about themselves. This is the heart of legalism—spiritual arrogance—spiritual blindness. Jesus advises, " 'I counsel you to buy from me gold refined in the fire, so you can become rich; and white clothes to wear, so you can cover your shameful nakedness; and salve to put on your eyes, so you can see' " (Revelation 3:18).

Gold is a faith that has been tested by trials. The white clothes are the garments of Christ's righteousness, not our own good deeds. Eye salve is the eye-opening work of the Holy Spirit. His first work is to show us our sinful condition and, therefore, our need of a Savior.

Jesus wants us to see our spiritual poverty and our need of the riches of Christ's sacrifice. And if we will do this, Jesus promises, " 'To him who overcomes, I will give the right to sit with me on my throne, just as I overcame and sat down with my Father on his throne' " (Revelation 3:21).

Spiritual arrogance must be cured by spiritual brokenness. We must see our desperate need and the abundant provision of Jesus for that need.

In the messages to the seven churches of Asia Minor, Jesus has outlined seven different spiritual conditions. Most likely you can see yourself in at least one of these seven spiritual conditions.

The message of Christ to us through the seven churches is this: regardless of where you are in your spiritual life, God loves you and accepts you and offers a promise to meet your most pressing need today.

The spiritual conditions represented by these seven churches are varied. Some are pretty good, but most are pretty bad. In each case, God claims those typified by each church as His children and longs to spend eternity with them.

Do not hesitate to come to Jesus because you feel you are too bad. Jesus has made provision for you, regardless of your sin, regardless of your condition, and regardless of how negatively you view yourself. Do not hesitate, but come to Him today, just as you are. He will not turn you away.

That's the message of Revelation here to us—to you, to me, and to Larry.

CHAPTER FOUR

The One Who Is Worthy

Revelation 4

Revelation 2 and 3 showed seven different spiritual conditions. With the exception of the churches at Smyrna and Philadelphia, those conditions were pitiful. Most Christians in the Western world would have to admit that their spiritual condition would best be described by one of the five churches—but not by Smyrna and Philadelphia.

What must happen to change this?

Throughout the book of Revelation I find an intriguing pattern. The pattern begins with a description of a crisis on earth and then heaven's response.

Some who teach from this book deal only with the crises on earth. They miss out, however, on the most important part of the book: heaven's response to those crises on earth.

Sandwiched between each crisis, John gives us a picture of how heaven responds to the crisis on earth. Heaven responds to earth's crises through the act of worship. A service of praise to God and to Jesus is the first response of heaven to any crisis. Heaven's answer to any crisis on earth is worship.

Our answer to a crisis in life should be worship as well. If we learned no other lesson from Revelation than this, we will have learned enough.

A Frenchman once commented that Americans have three idols: size, noise, and speed. Worship runs in the opposite direction. It does remind us of the greatness of God, but it also reminds us of just how small we are.

Worship is being still and knowing God. Worship is waiting upon the Lord. Worship helps us find who we are and why God has placed us here on the earth.

We can worry, or we can worship. Worship and worry cannot live in the same heart: They are mutually exclusive. But, strangely enough, busy people find it a whole lot easier to worry than to worship.

Fyodor Dostoevsky wrote, "The one essential condition of human existence is that man should always be able to bow down before something infinitely great. . . . The Infinite and the Eternal are as essential for man as the little planet on which he dwells."

God created us for the purpose of worshiping Him. If we haven't learned to worship, it doesn't matter how well we do anything else.

A.W. Tozer wrote, "We are called to an everlasting preoccupation with God."

What was Jesus thinking about as He walked along the roads of Galilee, so often alone? What were His thoughts in times of repose, during the journeys by boat that He liked making with His disciples after a day's exhausting preaching? What do you believe occupied His mind among the hills where He liked to go alone, without even the disciples?

We may think the answer to be easy: He was thinking of men, of sinners and their salvation, and what He had to do to effect that salvation. But surprising as it may seem to us, Jesus wasn't preoccupied with thoughts about us. The constant object of His meditation, the natural orientation of His heart and mind and soul, the food that constantly nourished Him, was His Father.

Jesus engaged in the act of worship as He walked along the Palestinian countryside. Jesus worshiped the Father in His thoughts and through prayer.

Worship is the highest and noblest act that any person can do. When men worship, God is satisfied! And when you worship, you are fulfilled!

True worship, however, does not just look at the acts of God in history. Worship is not primarily looking back. While looking back can be important because it reminds us that God has taken care of us in days past, it is not to be the only activity of worship. Worship should also focus on the present and the future.

When the Tennessee Valley Authority system created Watauga Lake in 1948, it buried the old community of Butler, Tennessee. In 1983, the water had to be lowered to repair the dam. Thousands of people waded through the mud to see where their homes once stood and to relive memories of the past.

Worship lets us relive memories of the past—not only our own personal past, but also the collective past of all the believers who have gone before us. But worship is more than sentiment or nostalgia. Worship looks to the future to inspire us to better deeds and better lives.

Our worship services today have basically three elements: praise, prayer, and preaching. Theologically and historically, worship is prayer. Our prayers ought to be the most exciting moments in worship. However, prayer is useful only for those who do not live in the constant physical presence of God. In heaven there will be no prayer because we will be in the presence of God. There will be no need to intercede or lay petitions before Him. Instead, in heaven there will be worship and continuous praise. Our occupation in heaven will be eternal praise for our gracious God and King.

Why will we spend the ceaseless ages of eternity praising God? We will praise the Father, Son, and Holy Ghost because in heaven, with nothing to obscure our view, we will see once and for all that They alone are worthy. Experiencing an unobstructed view of the Trinity, we will have only one response: heartfelt praise and worship.

Chapter 4 speaks of the worth of Jesus as the object of our worship.

It teaches us that the quality of our worship will be limitless because the worth of our Savior knows no limit. His value cannot be measured.

Let's look at heaven's response to the mess we find on earth. Heaven begins each worship service by acknowledging the worth of Jesus, our Savior. Let's begin with Revelation chapter 4. "After this I looked, and there before me was a door standing open in heaven. And the voice I had first heard speaking to me like a trumpet said, 'Come up here, and I will show you what must take place after this.' At once I was in the Spirit, and there before me was a throne in heaven with someone sitting on it. And the one who sat there had the appearance of jasper and carnelian. A rainbow, resembling an emerald, encircled the throne" (Revelation 4:1–3).

Immediately after showing John a vivid picture of a crisis of faith on earth, the next picture is the throne of God. The view appears to be bright, colorful, and glorious. "Surrounding the throne were twenty-four other thrones, and seated on them were twenty-four elders. They were dressed in white and had crowns of gold on their heads. From the throne came flashes of lightning, rumblings and peals of thunder. Before the throne, seven lamps were blazing. These are the seven spirits of God" (Revelation 4:4, 5).

Scholarly consensus (though not unanimous) on the meaning of the twenty-four elders is that they represent the church in both Old and New Testament times. The church in the Old Testament was represented by the twelve tribes of Israel, and in New Testament times by the twelve apostles. The fact that they are dressed in white and are wearing crowns suggests that they are humans who have overcome by the merits of Christ's righteousness.

The seven lamps are interesting. Seven is the number of completion or perfection. The passage tells us that this represents the "seven spirits of God." We can assume that the seven lamps represent the coming of the perfect ministry of the Holy Spirit to the world. It is only by the ministry of that Spirit that the spiritual condition of Christians will ever be improved.

The description continues:

> Also before the throne there was what looked like a sea of glass, clear as crystal.
>
> In the center, around the throne, were four living creatures, and they were covered with eyes, in front and in back. The first living creature was like a lion, the second was like an ox, the third had a face like a man, the fourth was like a flying eagle. Each of the four living creatures had six wings and was covered with eyes all around, even under his wings. Day and night they never stop saying:
>
> "Holy, holy, holy
>
> is the Lord God Almighty,
>
> who was, and is, and is to come" (Revelation 4:6–8).

The living creatures are most likely an exalted order of angels who continuously sing praise to God. Their wings tell us that they are swift as they carry out the will of God. These angels have many eyes all around their bodies. Eyes represent intelligence, discernment, and wisdom. Their song is "Holy, holy, holy is the Lord God Almighty."

Although Revelation was written in Greek, the idea contained in the song is taken from the Hebrew. In Hebrew, if an aspect of God's character is to be emphasized, it is repeated. To repeat something once means that it is really, really good. To repeat it twice is to take the thing to the third degree, which is the superlative. The holiness of God is greatly emphasized in this worship service. God is not just holy, and He is not just holy, holy; God is holy, holy, holy!

God is also said to be the One "who was, and is, and is to come." God is always present in all of time. He always has been, He always will be, and He most definitely is present today. He is the God of yesterday, today, and tomorrow.

The first 8 verses of chapter 4 are filled with God's praises. God is venerated as the most majestic, powerful, wise, and holy Being in the universe. Just describing God is an act of praise and worship!

Whenever the living creatures give glory, honor and thanks to him who sits on the throne and who lives for ever and ever, the twenty-four elders fall down before him who sits on the throne, and worship him who lives for ever and ever. They lay their crowns before the throne and say:

"You are worthy, our Lord and God,
  to receive glory and honor and power,
for you created all things,
  and by your will they were created
  and have their being" (Revelation 4:9–11).

The four living creatures are worshiping God with incredible enthusiasm. The twenty-four elders show Him complete devotion as they fall face down before Him, giving Him their crowns.

These crowns were given to these representatives of the Old and New Testament churches in recognition of their victory on earth. Now they are made rulers in heaven. But these twenty-four elders recognize that they have done nothing on their own. God alone is to receive glory, and so they cast their crowns before Him. After all, He is the One who has won the victory, even if it was through them.

During the time of the Roman Empire, whenever a king from a kingdom within the empire would come to Rome for an audience with Caesar, they would lay their crowns before him. Then they would address the emperor by saying, "You are worthy."

John wrote Revelation during the reign of Domitian, whose official title was "Our Lord and God." John reminds citizens of the Roman Empire that there is only One who is "Our Lord and God," and that is the God of heaven. He alone is worthy of that title; He alone is worthy of our praise.

The twenty-four elders declare that God alone is worthy to be called "Our Lord and God." They give their crowns to God in recognition of the fact that they could have done nothing without Him. They sing praises to God and refer to Him by the title "Our Lord and

God." The praise they give to God acknowledges that He is worthy to receive honor and power. He is worthy, they say, because He is the Creator and the Sustainer of all things.

The leaders of the Protestant Reformation understood this fact. The Reformation was based on five ideas, or doctrinal statements: Scripture alone, Christ alone, grace alone, faith alone, and glory to God alone.

The four creatures and the twenty-four elders demonstrate this important doctrine. They refuse to accept praise, but redirect all glory to God.

You have accomplishments in your life. Perhaps you have overcome great obstacles to find success. You may be proud of a happy family, a well-run business, or success in your chosen profession or career.

Revelation 4 tells us that whatever the accomplishment, only God is to receive glory. He alone is to be praised. On February 19, 2002, Vonetta Flowers made Olympic history. She became the first person of African descent—American or otherwise—to medal in the Winter Games when she and her teammate won the gold in the bobsled for the U.S.A. Vonetta became a celebrity. But in spite of all the attention lavished on her, Vonetta continued to say, "I thank God for this win, because without Him I wouldn't be here."

Vonetta was singled out at the age of nine as a track athlete with Olympic potential. "My first track coach, Dewitt Thomas, told me I could be the next Jackie Joyner-Kersee, and I believed him," she says. "But it was always the *summer* Olympics I pictured."

At the University of Alabama at Birmingham, Vonetta became one of the school's most decorated student athletes and the first person from her family to graduate from college. But when she tried out for the U.S. Olympic track and field team in 1996, ankle injuries caused her to finish in thirteenth place. Vonetta said, "I'd achieved a lot of success in track and field based on my individual efforts, and I believed if I trained hard enough and stayed healthy, that would be enough for me to make the Olympic team. I didn't yet realize I needed

God in my life to help me find my purpose and to understand that what He wanted for my life was far greater than anything I ever could have imagined."

The following year, she started attending church with a friend. At church Vonetta decided to accept Jesus as her personal Savior, and to follow Him by living a life of obedience to Him. Vonetta married and tried for the Olympic team again in 2000, but a back injury and ankle surgery kept her off the team. Her husband saw a flyer encouraging track and field athletes to try out for the bobsled team.

After years of training and disappointment, Vonetta ended up on Jill Bakken's team at the 2002 Winter Olympics in Salt Lake City. Vonetta says, "I just put my faith in God and let Him take over. I do my job of training and put the rest in His hands."

Whether you are in crisis or are celebrating some grand achievement, there can be only one appropriate response for a follower of Jesus Christ. We are to acknowledge the infinite worth of Jesus as the object of our praise. We are to worship Him as our Creator and our Redeemer.

His glory is our strength. His power is our assurance. His faithfulness is our comfort. Knowing this all to be true places our minds at ease. We can sleep at night because *Yahweh* is "Our Lord and God."

Chapter Five

The One Who Ensures Victory

Revelation 5

*B*efore the advent of the tape recorder, a man bought a machine that enabled him to cut his own records on discs. He listened to Winston Churchill's famous speech over the radio and recorded it. But the record cracked, and if you played it, you heard Churchill saying, "Our aim is victory, victory, victory, victory, victory, victory!"

When you read the book of Revelation, you seem to hear the word, like the refrain of a great hymn, over and over in the background: "Victory! Victory! Victory!" The battle has been fought, the war has been won. The victory parade is about to begin, and it will be grander than any New York ticker-tape version!

At the head of the parade will be Adam and Eve, as perfect as the day God first made them. They will be singing a song of victory—a song that gives honor and glory to the Hero of the war. They will be followed by a long parade of patriarchs: Abraham, Isaac, Jacob, and others. And these too will be singing the same song of redemption, which glorifies the One who has won the victory for us all.

Next will be prophets: Isaiah, Jeremiah, Daniel, Amos, Hosea, and so many more. Their voices will join the others as they sing of glory and honor to the Victor.

Old Testament kings such as David and Solomon will join the chorus of praise. Disciples will add a new verse as they sing of the climactic battle of the conflict. Matthew, John, James, and Peter will sing with the apostle Paul of the battles they witnessed together.

The great Reformers will sing of the wonderful things they witnessed during this inexorable march to victory. Men and women, boys and girls from every age will be a part of this parade—singing as they go—their joy uncontainable.

But finally, at the climax of the parade, in the featured spot, will appear the Hero—He who won the war for all of them.

He is known by many names: King of kings, Lord of lords, Redeemer, Savior, the Son of man, the Lion of the tribe of Judah, and the Lamb that was slain. But to the millions upon millions who worship, love, and adore Him, He is simply known as Jesus.

Jesus is the Hero of the war. Jesus is the One who won the victory! And Jesus wrote the words to the song sung by the participants of the parade—"Victory, Victory, Victory!"

A precursor to the great parade of victory is described in Revelation the fifth chapter. It is a worship service in heaven that celebrates the One who is worthy of such praise.

Revelation 5 continues the worship started in Revelation 4. The setting is a heavenly celebration of Christ's victory through His death, resurrection, and now His ascension.

This celebratory worship service took place just after the ascension of Christ, or about the time of Pentecost, when the disciples received the special outpouring of the Holy Spirit. Commentator Ranko Stefanovic tells us that the scene described in Revelation 4 and 5 is the worship service at the enthronement of Jesus after the Ascension.

Let's continue with this heavenly worship service. "Then I saw in the right hand of him who sat on the throne a scroll with writing on both sides and sealed with seven seals" (Revelation 5:1).

Ranko Stefanovic writes in his commentary on Revelation that when a king ascended to the throne in Israel, a special scroll was prepared for him. This was a scroll of the covenant between God and Israel. It was a new copy of Deuteronomy. It was expected that the king would read and study from this scroll every day.

Israel viewed the king to be a co-ruler of the nation, with God. When the king sat on the throne, he held the scroll in his hand as his scepter. His right to open the scroll and read it was a symbol of his authority to rule the nation as co-ruler with God.

Revelation 5 depicts God as holding a scroll that is sealed with seven seals. This scroll is the scroll of the covenant between God and His people. It symbolizes the right to rule.

Official documents in ancient times would bear an official seal. This seal was usually of wax and was placed on the rolled-up parchment, securing and closing the rolled scroll. When the king sealed a document, he made an impression in the wax, usually with his ring. This made a distinctive impression, easily recognized by everyone who saw the seal.

Only those authorized could open the seal. A person must be deemed worthy to break the seal and to read the scroll. "And I saw a mighty angel proclaiming in a loud voice, 'Who is worthy to break the seals and open the scroll?' But no one in heaven or on earth or under the earth could open the scroll or even look inside it. I wept and wept because no one was found who was worthy to open the scroll or look inside. Then one of the elders said to me, 'Do not weep! See, the Lion of the tribe of Judah, the Root of David, has triumphed. He is able to open the scroll and its seven seals' " (Revelation 5:2–5).

In Israel, the king was to be of the lineage of David. No one else was worthy to reign. John tells us that Jesus has the correct bloodline to rule. He is of the tribe of Judah, an offspring of David. Jesus is also qualified to reign since He alone has triumphed over sin and death. These things make Jesus worthy to open the seven seals from the scroll of the covenant and to read from them.

When John looks to see this "Lion of the tribe of Judah," he gets a surprise. Instead of a Lion, John sees a Lamb. "Then I saw a Lamb, looking as if it had been slain, standing in the center of the throne, encircled by the four living creatures and the elders. He had seven horns and seven eyes, which are the seven spirits of God sent out into all the earth" (Revelation 5:6).

Jesus is known by many titles. Here two are used: "the Lion of the tribe of Judah" and "the Lamb that has been slain."

I like the fact that one of the earliest entrances of Christ onto the stage of Revelation has Him entering as a "Lamb, looking as if it had been slain." One of the first things Jesus wants us to know about Himself is that He is our Savior. He is the One who died for our sins. He is the spotless Lamb of God who was foreshadowed by countless animal sacrifices. Jesus wants us to see Him as our Redeemer. That's the picture He wants to dominate our thoughts of Him. He is the Lamb that has been slain for our sins.

This Lamb has seven horns and seven eyes. Horns symbolize power or authority. The number seven is the number of perfection or completion. Jesus has perfect or complete authority to reign. Eyes represent intelligence, discernment, or wisdom. Seven eyes tell us that Jesus' wisdom is perfect. Jesus has the right and the wisdom necessary to reign supreme over the entire universe.

"He came and took the scroll from the right hand of him who sat on the throne" (Revelation 5:7). Since the scroll symbolizes the right and authority to reign over the entire universe, the fact that Jesus takes the scroll from God tells us that God has declared Jesus to be worthy to open and read the scroll. Jesus is worthy to reign over the universe. This scroll is the covenant that contains the terms and conditions of the promise of God to His people. That scroll tells us that if we accept Jesus as our Sovereign, He will grant us to be His children and will give us eternal life.

Jesus holds the scroll of the covenant in His hand, which means that He has the authority and the right to reign over you. Without the covenant promise made to you, Jesus cannot reign! His promised salvation is also His authority.

Do you think for one minute that Jesus will ever back out of His promise to grant to you eternal life? Of course not! That would mean that He was not worthy to reign as our Lord! To back out of the covenant promise would be to abdicate His throne.

> And when he had taken it, the four living creatures and the twenty-four elders fell down before the Lamb. Each one had a harp and they were holding golden bowls full of incense, which are the prayers of the saints. And they sang a new song:
>
> "You are worthy to take the scroll
>   and to open its seals,
> because you were slain,
>   and with your blood you purchased men for God
>   from every tribe and language and people and nation.
> You have made them to be a kingdom and priests to serve our God,
>   and they will reign on the earth" (Revelation 5:8–10).

The four living creatures, who are exalted angels, and the twenty-four elders, who are representatives from earth of those who have been saved throughout all time, fall at the feet of Jesus and sing praises to Him. They sing to the glory of the spotless Lamb of God, who alone is worthy to reign.

Jesus' sovereignty is sealed through His faithfulness to keep the terms of the covenant with you. Your promised salvation, the covenant, is Jesus' scepter. It is the symbol of His authority and power.

If you cannot sing about this, then you are not alive! If you have received the promise, then you must sing! We will live and reign with Jesus throughout eternity.

> Then I looked and heard the voice of many angels, numbering thousands upon thousands, and ten thousand times ten

thousand. They encircled the throne and the living creatures and the elders. In a loud voice they sang:

"Worthy is the Lamb, who was slain,
to receive power and wealth and wisdom and strength
and honor and glory and praise!" (Revelation 5:11, 12).

The song began with the four living creatures and the twenty-four elders. Now every angel of heaven joins the song. Angels do not benefit from the salvation that Jesus won at Calvary because they never sinned. These angels are singing about *your* salvation. They are singing about the worthiness of the Lamb of God to be the possessor of power, wealth, wisdom, strength, honor, glory, and praise.

Why? The angels sing because, through His personal sacrifice, Jesus has won your salvation. The angels look upon this act of love and are driven to sing. They must glorify the One who alone is worthy. They must praise the immeasurable love of the Lamb!

If the angels sing about your salvation, something from which they do not personally benefit, don't you think we should sing with even greater gusto songs of praise to the One who saved us? How can we go to church and mumble the words of our hymns and praise music when Jesus has won for us so great a salvation?

Then I heard every creature in heaven and on earth and under the earth and on the sea, and all that is in them, singing:

"To him who sits on the throne and to the Lamb
be praise and honor and glory and power,
for ever and ever!"

The four living creatures said, "Amen," and the elders fell down and worshiped (Revelation 5:13, 14).

The four living creatures and the twenty-four elders started the song. As they sang, the host of angels joined the chorus. The music grows, the volume swells until it reaches a glorious crescendo. But the song is not complete unless you are singing.

John has the inhabitants of earth joining the song. They sing, "To him who sits on the throne and to the Lamb be praise and honor and glory and power, for ever and ever!" Everyone in the universe worships the Lamb.

> "Worthy is the Lamb, who was slain,
> to receive power and wealth and wisdom and strength
> and honor and glory and praise!"

Prose is inadequate! This is poetry! Prose can never sufficiently praise God. Worship and praise require poets and musicians! It requires more than the expression of doctrinal truth. Worship must be an experience of the heart!

You cannot find a scriptural description of a worship service in heaven that does not include music. Music is essential if Jesus is to be praised properly.

Let's follow the example of Scripture today. Let's join the song begun by the four living creatures, the twenty-four elders, and the hosts of heaven.

It is time for earth to be involved. Let's join in the praise of Jesus by using the only language that is adequate to give expression to His glory. Let us sing to the glory of the Lamb!

CHAPTER SIX

The One Who Controls All Things

Revelation 6:1–8:1

*A*s a boy I would listen to preachers speak from Revelation who seemed especially interested in how the prophecies of Revelation related to the end of time and the second coming of Jesus. Because Revelation is filled with mysterious symbols that all seem to represent perilous times, the preachers would speak of natural disasters such as famines, earthquakes, and hail storms. They would also speak of war, persecution, martyrs, and terrible times of spiritual confusion.

Some were so skilled at painting a frightening picture that when I walked out of the church I expected to see persecutors and oppressors around every corner. I often wondered how I could ever face the terrible events that will precede the Second Coming. I feared, not primarily the coming of Jesus, but what would happen before!

First, what I didn't realize was that, though the preachers spoke as if certain what they were saying were true—a lot has proved, in fact, untrue. Many of the prophecies of Daniel and Revelation were, they said, to be fulfilled in powers like the Ottoman Empire and the Soviet Union. Obviously, those predictions were wrong.

I remember when prominent television evangelists predicted that terrible things would happen at midnight of December 31, 1999. You know: airplanes would fall from the sky, electric appliances would either stop working or else attack you, and computers would freeze or would destroy much of the economy of the world. Surely, they predicted, this would be the end of the world. The coming of Jesus, then, could not be far behind!

Wrong again! (How they continue to draw a following is beyond me, but some of the same people continue to tune them in every week and send them money every month!)

Also, I didn't realize that the most important message of Revelation regarding the end of the world is simply that if I am trusting in Jesus, I don't need to worry about the trials of the last days. Jesus is Sovereign—He is in control, and He will see me through. I can rest in His power.

In Revelation 4 and 5 we have witnessed a worship service in heaven that celebrated the enthronement of the risen Christ. Heaven and earth sang praises to the Lamb, for He alone is worthy to open the scroll and He alone is worthy to reign.

The scroll that Jesus is worthy to open is the scroll of the covenant. The covenant contains the terms by which men and women become the children of God and receive eternal life. God, through Jesus, has fulfilled all but one phase of His end of the bargain in the covenant. The only thing left for God to do is to come to take those who have accepted the terms of the covenant to live with Him in heaven.

In chapters 4 and 5, Jesus is about to break the seven seals and open the scroll of the covenant. Beginning with chapter 6, we have a description of the results of breaking the seals and opening the scroll. Opening the seals triggers events. These events take place beginning at the enthronement ceremony of Christ and continuing until the Second Coming.

I would like to focus on the first four seals now. The first four seals paint a vivid picture of the conditions on planet Earth between the first century and the Second Coming. These conditions have occurred throughout the Christian era and will continue until Jesus returns. "I watched as the Lamb opened the first of the seven seals. Then I heard one of the four living creatures say in a voice like thunder, 'Come!' I looked, and there before me was a white horse! Its rider held a bow, and he was given a crown, and he rode out as a conqueror bent on conquest" (Revelation 6:1, 2).

As Jesus opened the first seal, John saw a white horse. White horses are symbolic of a conqueror. The rider has a bow and wears a crown representing warfare and victory. The rider of the white horse represents the spreading of the gospel after Pentecost and down to this day. Through His faithful people who share the gospel message with everyone on the planet, Jesus is waging spiritual warfare against the forces of evil.

When Jesus opened the first seal, the Holy Spirit was poured out on the earth with great power. The first day of the manifestation of the Spirit's power saw three thousand new believers added to the church in Jerusalem. He brought miracle-working power to the disciples and conviction to their preaching. The gospel spread throughout the world with amazing speed.

That same Spirit is present in the earth today. He is just as capable of facilitating the gospel today as He was during the first century A.D. We can see Him at work in many parts of the world even now.

As I edit this chapter, I am at a theological seminary outside of Moscow, Russia. I am speaking to a group of fifteen hundred pastors faithfully working for the cause of Christ throughout Russia and the former Soviet block countries. Every meeting has been filled with stories of miracles that Jesus has performed for the victorious spread of the gospel. They tell of how God sustained them through the years of persecution under communism and how He continues to work miracles in the new challenges they face.

God is anxious to work where you live, right now. Jesus still defeats the forces of evil and allows the good news of the gospel to spread widely. "When the Lamb opened the second seal, I heard the second living creature say, 'Come!' Then another horse came out, a fiery red one. Its rider was given power to take peace from the earth and to make men slay each other. To him was given a large sword" (Revelation 6:3, 4).

We mentioned that the white horse represented victory in a spiritual conflict. The spiritual forces of evil are never happy with the success of the gospel, so Satan responds with a vicious counterattack. As the gospel spreads, persecution follows. Red is the color of blood—the blood of martyrs.

It is difficult for many of us in the Western world to realize that many are persecuted, even martyred, for the sake of Christ today. In the United States, we have taken our religious liberty for granted. Recently we have seen stories in the news about a man in Afghanistan who was imprisoned for having converted to Christianity. This man faced the possibility of death if convicted. After great political pressure, the man was released from prison. He promptly disappeared. Later it was learned that he had fled the country.

While this man's case made the news, we never hear about the countless other Christians in Muslim countries who have been imprisoned and even executed for their faith.

As I visit in Russia, I hear stories of imprisonment, torture, and even martyrdom for the cause of Christ as the people suffered under communism. As they tell the stories, tears fill their eyes. And yet, there is an enormous sense of joy at the fact that Jesus never left them. They look forward to a day when they will enjoy safety, freedom, joy, and everlasting life with the One who sustained them in times of trouble. Wherever the gospel is accepted, those who accept the gospel receive peace. When the gospel is rejected, persecution against those who accept the gospel follows.

Let's move on to the third seal.

"When the Lamb opened the third seal, I heard the third living creature say, 'Come!' I looked, and there before me was a black horse! Its rider was holding a pair of scales in his hand. Then I heard what sounded like a voice among the four living creatures, saying, 'A quart of wheat for a day's wages, and three quarts of barley for a day's wages, and do not damage the oil and the wine!' " (Revelation 6:5, 6).

Black, in Revelation, represents spiritual darkness. Darkness occurs when the gospel is not present. The balance refers to a time of famine or great scarcity, when it is difficult for people to acquire the basic necessities of life. So scarce are these basics that they must be carefully measured.

A quart of grain was the daily ration for a man. Barley was the cheapest of the grains available in Palestine, yet under the third seal it takes an entire day's wage to purchase the cheapest grain available and even then you could purchase only enough for one day. In times of plenty you might expect that your wage for the day could purchase twelve to fifteen quarts of barley. Thus, the time talked about here is a time of great scarcity.

Still, the voice declared that the oil and the wine would not be damaged. Even though a spiritual famine exists under this seal, these staples of life would remain available. The oil represents the Holy Spirit, while wine represents salvation through Jesus. Even in times of great spiritual famine, a famine of God's Word, salvation is still available to anyone who will receive it.

Now let's look at the fourth seal:

"When the Lamb opened the fourth seal, I heard the voice of the fourth living creature say, 'Come!' I looked, and there before me was a pale horse! Its rider was named Death, and Hades was following close behind him. They were given power over a fourth of the earth to kill by sword, famine and plague, and by the wild beasts of the earth" (Revelation 6:7, 8).

Death and Hades, the rider of the fourth horse, is given power over one fourth of the earth. This means that not only is his power limited but he has no power of his own. Power must be given to the rider of the pale horse.

Jesus, in Revelation 1:18, is said to have the keys to Death and Hades ("Hades," by the way, simply means "the grave"). Jesus has won the victory over Death and Hades. He was won the victory over the grave by His own death and resurrection. The only power death can have today is the power Christ allows it to have.

This is a precious promise to me. Through the decades of ministry, I have conducted several hundred funerals. I have attended over five

hundred deaths. At times, especially when working as a cha,
pital or hospice, I have been overwhelmed by the sheer volume ι

But Jesus has overcome death and the grave. Jesus has defea.
these seemingly invincible enemies and put them on a leash. Eventually, He will banish them from His kingdom altogether.

Under the fourth seal, the words *sword, famine, plague,* and *wild
beasts* are references from the Old Testament, whose writers used these
terms to refer to God's judgments—judgments designed to bring His
people to repentance.

This fourth seal simply describes what happens when the gospel is
rejected. Death results. This seal tells us that Jesus loves even those
who have rejected the gospel, and He attempts to bring them to repentance through His judgments.

What can we say about the first four of the seven seals? Commentator Ranko Stefanovic notes, "Clearly, the four horsemen of the first
four seals stand for the victorious spreading of the gospel and the con-
sequences of rejecting it."

It is true that Jesus is coming again, and until He comes, there will
be times of spiritual light and spiritual darkness, times of an abun-
dance of God's Word and times of a famine of God's Word, times of
safety and times of persecution and even martyrdom. But through it
all, Jesus is in control. He makes salvation available to all and has
promised to see you through to the end. You have no reason to fear:
Jesus is in control!

The fifth seal deals with God's love for those who have suffered for
His sake.

"When he opened the fifth seal, I saw under the altar the souls of
those who had been slain because of the word of God and the testimony they had maintained. They called out in a loud voice, 'How
long, Sovereign Lord, holy and true, until you judge the inhabitants
of the earth and avenge our blood?' Then each of them was given a
white robe, and they were told to wait a little longer, until the number
of their fellow servants and brothers who were to be killed as they had
been was completed" (Revelation 6:9–11).

All but one of the disciples suffered a martyr's death. Thousands of Christians gave their lives for the sake of the gospel during the reign of the Caesars. They were killed in the Colosseum as cheering crowds watched lions rip them apart or gladiators run them through with the sword or spear. Some were covered with tar, impaled on a large stake, set aflame, and used to light banquet halls so Caesar and his guests could enjoy their debauched party.

During a period of 1,260 years, beginning in A.D. 538, it is estimated by some historians that as many as fifty to eighty million Christians were martyred.

Even today, persecution and martyrdom are not uncommon in certain places. As I stated before, in communist and Muslim countries, those who convert to Christianity are constantly at risk. The blood of innocent men, women, and children shed over the ages cries out for justice.

John, in his vision, has them crying from the grave, "How long, Sovereign Lord, holy and true, until you judge the inhabitants of the earth and avenge our blood?"

This is not just a plea for vengeance against those who so violently and unjustly took the lives of these dear saints, but it's also a cry that God be vindicated. The martyrs placed their faith in Him, trusting Him with their lives. Now they plead that the God they trusted be vindicated in order to demonstrate that their lives had not been wasted—that all see that their blood had not been shed in vain.

John said that they were given a white robe. White robes symbolize the covering we receive by faith as we accept Christ's forgiveness—we receive His robe of righteousness.

When, in faith, we accept Jesus as our Lord and Savior, we receive the benefits of His perfect life. We are granted eternal life, not based on our own good works, but based on Jesus' own perfect obedience of the law of God. We receive salvation because Jesus lived a perfect life, and because He suffered and died.

The martyrs are pictured as being covered with Christ's perfect life—His white robe of righteousness. They are told that there were to be more martyrs, and that some were being prepared, or perfected, for that very purpose.

I do not know if I will ever be called upon to give my life for the sake of Jesus, but others live under the constant threat of imprisonment, torture, or even death as a result of their faith in Jesus.

We should pray for these dear fellow believers, and pray that should God ever call upon us to make the ultimate sacrifice, we will—by God's grace—remain faithful.

What happens next?

> I watched as he opened the sixth seal. There was a great earthquake. The sun turned black like sackcloth made of goat hair, the whole moon turned blood red, and the stars in the sky fell to earth, as late figs drop from a fig tree when shaken by a strong wind. The sky receded like a scroll, rolling up, and every mountain and island was removed from its place.
>
> Then the kings of the earth, the princes, the generals, the rich, the mighty, and every slave and every free man hid in caves and among the rocks of the mountains. They called to the mountains and the rocks, "Fall on us and hide us from the face of him who sits on the throne and from the wrath of the Lamb! For the great day of their wrath has come, and who can stand?" (Revelation 6:12–17).

In the Old Testament, God's visit to earth is announced by earthquakes. The earth is being prepared for just such a visit, the second coming of Jesus. Our planet is reeling, just as a woman's body is racked with pain in childbirth.

The signs described here remind us that the things Jesus predicted would happen prior to His return. We find these things in Matthew 24 and 25, Mark 13, and Luke 21.

But not everyone is anxious for the Lord's visit to our planet. Verses 15 through 17 describe those who have not accepted the gospel. They attempt to hide themselves from the possibility of judgment at the hands of a just God. They fear that they are about to receive their just desserts; they are not anxious to stand before a holy God.

Those who have accepted the gospel have a different reaction. They know that they have been saved by the suffering and sacrifice of Jesus. They have nothing to fear—not because they have saved themselves (an impossibility, anyway) but simply because they have received the gospel and trusted in the merits of Christ. They are depicted in Scripture as welcoming Jesus with the words "This is our God and He will save us."

The gospel notes the difference in the reaction of these two groups to the Lord's coming. Those who have received the gospel will welcome Jesus; those who have not received it will react with fear at His return.

The sixth seal sounds ominous. It tells of tumultuous events on earth. How does heaven react to a crisis on earth?

Chapter 7 answers our question. It describes a pause in the winds of strife that precede the end of the world. These winds are being held back until God's people can be prepared. While this pause takes place, heaven answers the turmoil of earth by having a worship service.

> After this I looked and there before me was a great multitude that no one could count, from every nation, tribe, people and language, standing before the throne and in front of the Lamb. They were wearing white robes and were holding palm branches in their hands. And they cried out in a loud voice:

> "Salvation belongs to our God,
> who sits on the throne,
> and to the Lamb."

> All the angels were standing around the throne and around the elders and the four living creatures. They fell down on their faces before the throne and worshiped God, saying:

"Amen!
Praise and glory
and wisdom and thanks and honor
and power and strength
be to our God for ever and ever.
Amen!" (Revelation 7:9–12).

Chapter 7 answers the last question of chapter 6, "For the great day of their wrath has come, and who can stand?"

Who will stand in the day of judgment? Those who receive salvation from the Lamb will stand. All those whose clothing has been washed white in the blood of the Lamb will come through persecution and privation. They will never hunger again, and never thirst again; they belong to Jesus. They may have known sorrow and grief on this earth, but " 'God will wipe away every tear from their eyes' " (Revelation 7:17).

Here, heaven gives the proper response to the events on earth. God's people respond to a crisis through worship. We worship the Lamb—we worship our God.

It's just too simple for some, isn't it? But the truth is always simple—simple, yet profound. Worship is the answer to crisis, suffering, death, disease, rejection, and pain.

Now let's turn to the seventh seal. "When he opened the seventh seal, there was silence in heaven for about half an hour" (Revelation 8:1).

Why is there silence in heaven? There is silence in heaven because heaven is empty. Jesus told those who murdered them that the next time they saw Him He would be in the clouds of glory, accompanied by all the hosts of heaven. When Jesus comes again, He will bring with Him the Father and the Holy Spirit, and all the angels of heaven.

If you were an angel in heaven and had witnessed everything since the time of Lucifer's rebellion, the fall of Adam and Eve, and everything up through the crucifixion of Jesus, would you want to just wait in heaven for Jesus to bring the redeemed home with Him? Absolutely not! Every being in heaven longs to accompany Jesus when He returns to this earth in power and great glory.

Why is Jesus coming? He told us why: " 'Do not let your hearts be troubled. Trust in God; trust also in me. In my Father's house are many rooms; if it were not so, I would have told you. I am going there to prepare a place for you. And if I go and prepare a place for you, I will come back and take you to be with me that you also may be where I am' " (John 14:1–3).

Jesus will return in power and glory. He will avenge the blood of the martyrs and punish those who have rejected Him and persecuted His followers. He will rid this earth of sin, disease, death, grief, pain, suffering, war, and everything evil. But most of all, Jesus is coming to get you. He never wants to be separated from you again, and He never will be.

The seven seals show us the things that happen as a result of the preaching of the gospel. Some receive it and some do not. Some find salvation and peace, and others react with violence against those who accept Christ.

War, natural disasters, and other cataclysmic events take place, but those who receive the gospel have nothing to fear. Our God is in control and ultimately will triumph.

Jesus is coming for you. Don't you want to meet Him? You do if you've accepted the gospel. Prepare yourself for that event today by confessing your sins and receiving His forgiveness and salvation today.

There is no fear for those who trust Jesus; there is only joyous expectancy.

The One Who Dries Your Tears

Revelation 7:9–17

*H*ave you ever examined amber? Amber used to be called "the tears of the sea" because those lovely tear-shaped gems were found in the cold waters of the North Sea.

Rain has been referred to as tears. When it rained, poets used to say "the heavens wept."

The truth is, the heavens don't cry. People do. All over the world, at any given moment, some folks are crying, needing the comfort of God's presence, the comfort of faith, the comfort of grace.

What are your sorrows, the losses and fears and pains that keep you awake at night and cast a pale of sorrow and despair over your days?

Everyone has or has had sorrows. It is a part of being human. And when sorrows come, they seem to come all at once. As someone wrote, "When sorrows come, they come not single spies, but in battalions!"

Yes, we all have sorrows of one kind or another.

For ace relief pitcher Donnie Moore it was losing an American League championship game. In a moment of total torment, he shot his wife and then himself.

What do you grieve over? What causes you to weep?

A Chinese proverb states, "A day of sorrow is longer than a month of joy." For those who grieve, it certainly feels that way, doesn't it?

Few things in life will have a greater impact on a person than the experience of significant loss. Hospitalization for those in acute grief is 600 percent higher than for others in their particular risk group. The divorce rate for married couples increases dramatically when a child dies. The divorce rate for such couples during the first twelve to eighteen months after the death is 50 to 70 percent. Over a five-year period it is 95 percent!

The average recovery time from a significant loss is one to two years, although it is not uncommon for it to last three to five years. Symptoms include things like changes in appetite, somatic disturbances, short-term memory loss, inability to concentrate, uncontrollable weeping, and a loss of the will to live. Author Edgar Jackson poignantly describes grief:

> Grief is a young widow trying to raise her three children, alone. Grief is the man so filled with shocked uncertainty and confusion that he strikes out at the nearest person. Grief is a mother walking daily to a nearby cemetery to stand quietly and alone a few minutes before going about the tasks of the day. She knows that a part of her is in the cemetery, just as part of her is in her daily work. Grief is silent, knife-like terror and sadness that comes a hundred times a day, when you start to speak to someone who is no longer there. Grief is the emptiness that comes when you eat alone after eating with another for many years.
>
> Grief is teaching yourself to go to bed without saying good night to the one who had died. Grief is the helpless wishing that things were different when you know they are not and never will be again. Grief is a whole cluster of adjustments, apprehensions, and uncertainties that strike life in its forward progress and make it difficult to redirect the energies of life.

Grief and tears are common. You do not have to live long before you experience your own. Remember that the most perfect being who ever lived was called the Man of Sorrows.

We grieve for a variety of reasons besides death. There is also divorce; loss of health; loss of a job or career; amputation or mastectomy; loss of independence; or a loss of innocence and security through rape, incest, or other physical attack.

There is another grief often neglected—the grief caused by our own sins. A sorrow for sins can cause us to weep over things we wish we had not done or said. Guilt and regret cause tremendous grief!

Believe it or not, grief is not all bad. Grief enables us to, eventually, let go of the past and reach for God's glorious tomorrow. Sorrow has a way of purifying and ennobling the soul. What soap is for the body, tears are for the soul.

Meister Eckhart, who lived in the thirteenth and fourteenth centuries, said, "Sorrow is the root of all virtue."

Henry Ward Beecher wrote, "We are never ripe till we have been made so by suffering."

Sorrow is our John the Baptist, clad in grim garments, with rough arms, a son of the wilderness, baptizing us with bitter tears, preaching repentance; and behind him comes the gracious, affectionate, healing Lord, speaking peace and joy to the soul.

Grief is the vehicle that carries us from where we are to where we want to be. It carries us from the initial shock of the loss, through the months of pain and sorrow, all the way to recovery, renewal, and relief. And, in the process, we grow. We are purified and strengthened.

Only when grief finds its work done can God dispense us from it. Trial then stops only when it is useless; that is why it scarcely ever stops.

What do you grieve over? What causes you to cry?

John the revelator cried when he thought that no one would be found who was worthy to open the seals and read the book that was in the right hand of God. This book was the book of the covenant. It was the book of promise that God would guide, protect, and save those who trust Him. What a loss it would have been if the seals could not be opened and the covenant was left unfulfilled! So, when heaven was searched and no one was found to be worthy, John wept.

John's sorrow was ended when it was announced to him that the Lion of the tribe of Judah was worthy. And John looked and saw a Lamb as it had been slain. Jesus, who is both the Lion and the Lamb, is worthy. This turned John's tears into laughter, and a service of worship and praise broke out in heaven.

We studied this service in Revelation 4 and 5. In chapters 5 and 6, Jesus opens the seals of the book and fulfills the covenant, but before the covenant promise can be completely fulfilled, John sees a confusing morass of different-colored horses, of lightning and thunder, of Death and Hades, earthquakes, astronomical phenomena, blood, and winds of strife. All in all, a disturbing picture of wars, persecutions, and trials. The entire earth shakes with turmoil as Satan unleashes his wrath against the saints of God and God prepares to enter the final conflict with Satan.

John realized that great and terrible days lay ahead for the church. How would God's people survive? Was it possible for anyone to remain faithful?

And then, seemingly in answer to John's unasked question, Heaven gives its answer. Once again, in the face of all the terrible things that must come to pass, a service of worship and praise to God breaks out in heaven.

> After this I looked and there before me was a great multitude that no one could count, from every nation, tribe, people and language, standing before the throne and in front of the Lamb. They were wearing white robes and were holding palm branches in their hands. And they cried out in a loud voice:

> "Salvation belongs to our God,
> who sits on the throne,
> and to the Lamb."

> All the angels were standing around the throne and around the elders and the four living creatures. They fell

down on their faces before the throne and worshiped God, saying:

> "Amen!
> Praise and glory
> and wisdom and thanks and honor
> and power and strength
> be to our God for ever and ever.
> Amen!" (Revelation 7:9–12).

Inhabitants of heaven and saints on earth anticipate the eventual victory. How? With a service of praise and a song of victory. How will the church survive? Through the sustaining power of God. They don't need to have the strength to endure—God has enough strength for all. It is by His might that the saints gain the victory.

The scene continues:

> Then one of the elders asked me, "These in white robes— who are they, and where did they come from?"
> I answered, "Sir, you know."
> And he said, "These are they who have come out of the great tribulation; they have washed their robes and made them white in the blood of the Lamb" (Revelation 7:13, 14).

Victory comes through the blood of the Lamb! Victory does not come through the efforts of the saints, but through the blood of Jesus.

How did the Christians endure persecution, torture, and death? Did they endure because they were strong? Did they endure because there was something special about them?

No. They endured trial and terror by the blood of the Lamb. Salvation comes as a gift from the hand of Jesus Himself! The white robe of Christ's righteousness is ours as a gift because of the blood of the Lamb.

73

How will you survive persecution and trial? Will it be through your own efforts? No. It will come through trusting in the merits of Christ.

How will you prepare for the second coming of Jesus? By learning to trust in the blood of the Lamb. That's the only way.

Victory has to do with what Jesus has already done on Calvary's tree. Victory has little to do with you and everything to do with Jesus.

The scene in heaven continues as the elder explains the benefits for those who learn to trust in the blood of the Lamb.

> Never again will they hunger;
>   never again will they thirst.
> The sun will not beat upon them,
>   nor any scorching heat.
> For the Lamb at the center of the throne will be their
>   shepherd;
>   he will lead them to springs of living water.
> And God will wipe away every tear from their eyes
>   (Revelation 7:16, 17).

Every saint of God has wept bitter tears. They have wept over the loss of their loved ones—some even through persecution, torture, and murder. They have wept at their own pain. Tears have filled their eyes over separation from other believers. They have wept over their own sins and the sins of the world.

Weeping is a common occupation for the saints. In fact, it could be said that the saints became saints through their tears. Tears clean the windows of the soul.

Tears teach us wisdom that no book of philosophy can. Tears speak more eloquently than ten thousand tongues. Tears may be God's best gift to suffering man. It is through sorrow and tears that God perfects the saints. The tears of God's people are holy. Charles Dickens wrote, "We need never be ashamed of our tears, for they are rain upon the blinding dust of earth, overlying our hard hearts."

Through our tears, we discover lasting inner peace. Lucius Annaeus Seneca, a contemporary of Jesus, said, "Let tears flow of their own accord: their flowing is not inconsistent with inward peace and harmony."

Through tears, God brings us closer to each other. Tears teach us to care for the pain of others. Eleanor Roosevelt said, "To live through a period of stress and sorrow with another human being creates a bond which nothing seems able to break."

Through tears we find our comfort and hope in Christ. Oswald Chambers wrote, "There is only one being who can satisfy the last aching abyss of the human heart, and that is the Lord Jesus Christ."

Sorrow today helps us appreciate times of joy tomorrow. The deeper sorrow carves into your being, the more joy you can contain. Joy and sorrow are inseparable. Tears of separation make us yearn for the day of reunion. And tears that are the fruit of heartfelt sorrow for sin drive us to our knees in repentance. Repentant tears wash out the stain of guilt.

Tears are God's gift to man. On this earth, we were made for tears.

There are times when God asks nothing of his children except silence, patience, and tears. Our hearts were made to be broken.

In the classic film *The Wizard of Oz,* the wizard says to the Tin Man, "Hearts will never be practical until they can be made unbreakable."

Wrong! The fact that hearts are fragile makes them practical. Unless a heart is broken, there is no genuine sorrow for sin—no confession, no repentance, no turning from sin, and hence no forgiveness.

There is an ancient tale about a young woman who was expelled from heaven and told that she would be readmitted if she would bring back the one gift God valued the most.

The woman searched the earth and brought back some drops of blood from a dying patriot. She collected coins given by a destitute widow for the poor. She brought back a remnant of a Bible used by an eminent preacher. The woman even brought back the dust from the shoes of missionaries who served many years in a distant land.

According to the legend, although she brought back these things and more, each time she was turned back.

One day as she watched a small boy playing by a fountain, she saw a man ride up on horseback and dismount to take a drink. When he saw the boy playing, he thought of his own childhood innocence. But he looked into the water of the fountain and saw a reflection of his own hardened face. He was overcome by the sin in his life, and in that moment, he wept tears of repentance.

The young woman took one of those tears back to heaven, where she was received with joy.

Tears are God's gift to man. On this earth, we need tears. Tears and sorrows purify and perfect us. Sorrow for sin drives us to our knees and to God. On this earth, we need the precious gift of tears.

However, the day is coming when the gift of tears will no longer be necessary. In the presence of God, tears will be banished. God Himself will wipe the tears away from our eyes.

Earth has no sorrow that Heaven cannot heal. The divine Alchemist can miraculously change a sorrowing heart of lead into a golden mellowness that sings praises through tears.

Who dries the tears from your eyes? What do you do with the tears of repentance? When the Holy Spirit speaks to your heart about sin in your life, and you weep the tears of sorrow for sin, what happens to those tears? John says, "If we confess our sins, He is faithful and just to forgive us our sins and to purify us from all unrighteousness."

God will wipe the tears of repentance from your eyes today through His gift of grace. As God forgives you, He takes away your sorrow. And ultimately, when you are privileged to live in His presence in heaven, God will take from you even the memory of your transgressions. God will wipe the tears of sorrow for sin from your eyes, and you will never sin again.

What do you do with your grief? How do you handle your sorrow? Who dries the tears from your eyes?

Lewis and Doris wanted a child. For the first decade of their marriage, they hoped passionately for a child. They wanted a child more than they wanted anything else in the world. So they hoped and prayed for ten long years.

Finally, after ten years, Doris became pregnant. They thanked God and drank a toast to hope.

One night, about six months into the pregnancy, something went wrong, and Lewis called the doctor. The doctor told them that Doris was going into labor. They were to get her to the emergency room now.

"I'll meet you there," he said. "Oh, yes; I have one more thing to tell you; I should have told you before. Your baby is going to be seriously malformed."

"Malformed? Seriously? How serious?"

"Very serious. It's up to you now to tell Doris on the way to the hospital."

Lewis told her, but they decided that they were not going to give up hope. No matter what the doctor said, they were not going to give up hope. So they kept on hoping all through the night.

At six o'clock in the morning, the doctor came to Lewis with a somewhat embarrassed grin from ear to ear. He said, "Congratulations! You have a perfect boy. Come and see."

Lewis went with him, and there he was, yelling his head off, looking just like his dad—a perfect man-child. Lewis and Doris praised God!

It's true. Never give up hope. Never, ever give up hope.

But two days later their baby was dead. Hope can break your heart.

Lewis and Doris cried tears of sorrow. They grieved desperately. How could this have happened? But still, they decided not to give up hope.

Lewis and Doris are claiming the promise of a resurrection. Paul's words to the church at Thessalonica have taken on new meaning to them.

DEATH

Brothers, we do not want you to be ignorant about those who fall asleep, or to grieve like the rest of men, who have no hope. We believe that Jesus died and rose again and so we believe that God will bring with Jesus those who have fallen asleep in him. According to the Lord's own word, we tell you that we who are still alive, who are left till the coming of the Lord, will certainly not precede those who have fallen asleep. For the Lord himself will come down from heaven, with a loud command, with the voice of the archangel and with the trumpet call of God, and the dead in Christ will rise first. After that, we who are still alive and are left will be caught up together with them in the clouds to meet the Lord in the air. And so we will be with the Lord forever. Therefore encourage each other with these words (1 Thessalonians 4:13–18).

Lewis and Doris are comforted by the thought that one day soon, God Himself will wipe the tears from their eyes as they are reunited with their baby.

Does God dry the tears of grief from your eyes? Will you be a part of the reunion on resurrection morning? Are there loved ones you are longing to see on that day? Will you be there to see them?

If you wear a robe so white that no laundry soap could ever whiten it because it is made white by being washed in the blood of the Lamb, you will be there. You will be reunited with your loved ones.

God Himself will take His hand and gently caress your face. With His fingers He will dab away the tears from your eyes. And as He touches you, somehow you will know that you will never weep again. For God has taken away your sorrow—sorrow for sin and sorrow over the losses of life. In heaven, sorrow is forever banished!

Suddenly, you will be surprised by the sound of your own voice singing with the innumerable, white robed hosts, saying, "Amen! Blessing and glory and wisdom, thanksgiving and honor and power and might, be to our God forever and ever. Amen."

CHAPTER EIGHT

The One Who Defends You

Revelation 8:2–11:19

*E*very day when Bobby walked from home to his fourth-grade classroom, three large boys from the sixth grade would accost him. They roughed Bobby up, spilled his books on the ground, made disparaging remarks, and took any money he had. Though thoroughly humiliated, Bobby felt helpless to do anything. He was simply too embarrassed to tell anyone what was happening.

Bobby's older brother, Tim, was seventeen and a student at the high school. Suspicious, he began to probe and, eventually, Bobby poured out the whole story.

Tim then encouraged Bobby to stand up to the bullies.

"But they'll kill me! I'm gonna' get creamed!"

Tim told Bobby that bullies are basically cowards who always choose younger, smaller kids to pick on, and once challenged, they usually back down. Bobby agreed reluctantly that he would stand up to the bullies the next morning but was certain that this could be the last day of his young life.

Bobby then headed out for school the next day, feeling as if he were marching to his execution. Unbeknownst to Bobby, Tim followed close behind but out of sight. Then, as usual, the bullies jumped out and said, "Give us your money." This time Bobby said, "No! Get out of my way!"

To his amazement, the boys stood aside and allowed Bobby to walk by, leaving Bobby feeling ten feet tall.

What Bobby didn't know is that the bullies had been startled by the sight of Tim stepping out of the bushes behind Bobby, with a menacing look on his face. The boys stepped aside out of fear of retribution from Bobby's older brother.

Revelation tells us that a day is coming when the bullies who have persecuted, tortured, and even martyred God's people will receive retribution—not from God's people, but from their elder Brother, Jesus.

We are about to examine a portion of Revelation called the seven trumpets. This section of the book deals with those who have rejected the gospel, or have persecuted God's people, or participated in the crucifixion of Jesus. It speaks of the retribution they so richly deserve.

In these next chapters, God is portrayed as your Defender. The seven trumpets depict God's interventions in history as He judges those who have bullied God's people.

In Scripture, trumpets are used to announce God's arrival. They also serve as a reminder that God remembers you even when you are oppressed. He promises to protect and deliver you.

In Revelation 6:10, John depicts the souls of those who have been martyred as crying out for justice. "How long, Sovereign Lord, holy and true, until you judge the inhabitants of the earth and avenge our blood?"

The seven trumpets are God's answer to the martyrs' cry. Let's examine those trumpets.

> And I saw the seven angels who stand before God, and to them were given seven trumpets. Another angel, who had a golden censer, came and stood at the altar. He was given much incense to offer, with the prayers of all the saints, on the golden altar before the throne. The smoke of the incense, together with the prayers of the saints, went up before God from the

angel's hand. Then the angel took the censer, filled it with fire from the altar, and hurled it on the earth; and there came peals of thunder, rumblings, flashes of lightning and an earthquake (Revelation 8:2–5).

Every day in Israel's temple service, a morning and an evening sacrifice were offered on the altar of burnt offering in the temple courtyard. After making this sacrifice, the priest took a golden censer with incense back into the temple. There, he offered the incense on the altar of incense in the compartment called the Holy Place.

When the priest came out of the temple, he blessed the people who had been waiting outside. Seven priests blew seven trumpets, thus marking the end of the daily sacrifices. This ceremony served as a daily reminder to Israel that salvation was always available, and that their prayers had been heard.

Revelation 8 signifies that the prayers of God's people are about to be answered. God is about to respond to the cries of His covenant people, especially those who have been persecuted. He is about to judge their oppressors in fulfillment of His promise to defend His people. "The first angel sounded his trumpet, and there came hail and fire mixed with blood, and it was hurled down upon the earth. A third of the earth was burned up, a third of the trees were burned up, and all the green grass was burned up" (Revelation 8:7).

Hail, fire, and blood are symbols of God's judgment against the enemies of His people, while trees and grass usually represent God's people. Verse 7 suggests that those of God's people who have opposed the gospel are about to be punished.

Because the trumpets begin at the same point as the seven seals, we know that this blast begins with the crucifixion of Jesus. Therefore, this is God's judgment upon the leaders of Israel who participated in the crucifixion of Jesus and thus rejected the Messiah.

The second trumpet follows closely.

"The second angel sounded his trumpet, and something like a huge mountain, all ablaze, was thrown into the sea. A third of the sea turned into blood, a third of the living creatures in the sea died, and a third of the ships were destroyed" (Revelation 8:8, 9).

Because a mountain usually represents a nation or empire, and because this is a great mountain, we can assume that it represents a great empire. This trumpet is most likely a judgment against the Roman Empire. The turning of the sea to blood and the destruction of ships represent the eventual downfall and ruin of the Roman Empire's economy.

The first two trumpets, therefore, deal with the two nations who participated in the crucifixion of Jesus. They also conspired together to prevent or retard the spread of the gospel, and therefore received God's judgment.

Now comes the third trumpet.

"The third angel sounded his trumpet, and a great star, blazing like a torch, fell from the sky on a third of the rivers and on the springs of water—the name of the star is Wormwood. A third of the waters turned bitter, and many people died from the waters that had become bitter" (Revelation 8:10, 11).

The great, burning star that fell from the sky is a clear reference to Lucifer, who was cast out of heaven due to his rebellion. Rivers and springs of water always represent truth and salvation.

Jesus declared that He is the "Living Water." Without Jesus, our Living Water, we die spiritually, and eventually even physically.

Satan is pictured as polluting the rivers and springs of water. They are turned bitter by "Wormwood." Wormwood was a name given to a class of bitter herbs thought poisonous. Wormwood, according to John, turned the waters bitter, causing many people to die.

After the fall of the Roman Empire, the world plunged into what historians have referred to as the Dark Ages. This was a time when many false doctrines entered the church. The gospel was polluted and perverted, causing many souls to perish. During this time, the Bible was replaced with tradition and the teachings of men. Few understood the simplicity of the gospel. The face of God was hidden from the earth. It was a time of great apostasy. Those who drank from these bitter waters died a spiritual death. This woe is pronounced upon Satan and those who participated in the apostasy of the church.

Next, we find the fourth trumpet, now in verse 12. "The fourth angel sounded his trumpet, and a third of the sun was struck, a third of the moon, and a third of the stars, so that a third of them turned dark. A third of the day was without light, and also a third of the night" (Revelation 8:12).

The sun, moon, and stars going dark announce God's coming judgment. After the Dark Ages, the false doctrines that entered the church continued to have a devastating effect. God countered this darkness with the light of the Reformation. A wonderful revival spread across the earth. The gospel was once again announced in clear terms. Salvation was understood to be a free gift of God's grace, and Scripture was studied and cherished. However, in the years that followed the glory of the Reformation, false doctrines and heresies entered even Protestant churches.

After Satan attempted to pervert and destroy the gospel through the darkness of the Dark Ages, he employed a different tactic. Through the Age of Enlightenment, Satan attempted to change the thinking of earth's inhabitants, including that of Christians. In spite of the many positive things the Enlightenment brought to society, its negative effect on Christianity was to replace the authority of Scripture with intellectualism and reason. These became the new ultimate standards of truth, instead of the clear teachings of the Bible. The church reverted to little more than mere formalism, thus obliterating the light of the gospel. Darkness once again covered the earth.

The first four trumpets announce God's displeasure with those who work against the purity of the gospel. They chronicle God's judgment against those who oppose Him and who oppress His people. The bullies finally get their just rewards as God exercises His responsibilities as your Defender.

God will not allow those who persecute His people to go unpunished. But God is anxious that even those who persecute His people would tomorrow become true followers of Jesus.

Saul of Tarsus was a passionate enemy of those Jews who had become followers of Jesus. He had them arrested, jailed, and even executed until that day on the road to Damascus when a bright light blinded Saul, who then heard a voice crying out, "Saul, why are you persecuting Me?"

God had pronounced judgment upon Saul, a persecutor of His people. But God was anxious that Saul repent and turn to Him. Saul repented, God renamed him Paul, and God's judgments had served their purpose.

The judgments we find in Revelation are intended to serve the same purpose. God is calling those who persecute His people to come to repentance. God does not desire that any should perish but that all should come to salvation. However, when rebellion persists, God will execute judgment.

Now we turn to the fifth trumpet, but first, at the close of chapter 8, a triple woe is pronounced on those who refuse the warning of the final three angels. "As I watched, I heard an eagle that was flying in midair call out in a loud voice: 'Woe! Woe! Woe to the inhabitants of the earth, because of the trumpet blasts about to be sounded by the other three angels!' " (Revelation 8:13).

Biblical prophets pronounced blessings and curses upon people. A curse was called a "woe." A threefold divine woe is about to be pronounced upon those who reject the gospel. You will remember that in Scripture, superlatives are expressed by repetition. Here we have a prophetic woe taken to the third degree. This is the worst of all possible woes!

Remember that the judgments of the seven trumpets are not directed at you. They are aimed at those who have rejected the gospel. If you have been saved by His grace, you have nothing to fear from these judgments. Those who oppose the gospel, or persecute the people of God, have everything to fear from them if they fail to repent.

Let's look at the fifth trumpet as we turn to chapter 9.

The fifth angel sounded his trumpet, and I saw a star that had fallen from the sky to the earth. The star was given the key to the shaft of the Abyss. When he opened the Abyss, smoke rose from it like the smoke from a gigantic furnace. The sun and sky were darkened by the smoke from the Abyss. And out of the smoke locusts came down upon the earth and were given power like that of scorpions of the earth. They were told not to harm the grass of the earth or any plant or tree, but only those people who did not have the seal of God on their foreheads (Revelation 9:1–4).

The star that fell from heaven is most likely the same star we saw in the third trumpet. This is Lucifer, the former covering cherub who rebelled against God.

Lucifer is given the key to the abyss. The abyss came to be known as the place where Satan and his demons were confined.

Jesus holds the keys to the abyss and has restricted the influence Satan and his host could have on the earth. With the sounding of the fifth trumpet, Jesus allows Satan more freedom to do his dirty work on earth.

Sometimes we speak of giving someone enough rope to hang himself, meaning that if you give evil people enough freedom they will eventually cause their own ruin. They simply cannot help themselves. Their greed, anger, and lust are too strong for them to control. Eventually, they will give in to their dark side, and that will be their own undoing. That is exactly what Jesus is doing here with Satan and the forces of hell. He partially removes His controlling hand from them and allows them enough freedom to show their true colors.

The smoke that arises from the abyss is another symbol of judgment. As the smoke rises, it partially obliterates the light of the sun. Spiritual darkness falls on the earth. In verse 3 the smoke from the abyss is partially made up of locusts, another symbol of judgment. Locusts devour plant life and torment people. These locusts have the power of scorpions, a biblical symbol of demonic activity. Verse 11 tells us that their leader, or king, is none other than Satan himself.

Therefore, the fifth trumpet speaks of a plague of demonic forces that obliterate the light of the gospel as we near the end of this world. These forces may exhibit themselves through institutions or individuals, but their effect is devastating.

Later, John gives a detailed description of the locusts and the harm they do. It is obvious that the destruction they pour out on the earth is not military, but spiritual. The result is spiritual darkness. Notice, however, that the power of the locusts was limited. They could not hurt the grass or the plants, which are symbols for God's people. The locusts could harm only those who do not have God's seal—only those who are not God's children.

The people of God will suffer persecution from this plague, but it will not destroy them. While the thought of persecution is disquieting, the message of Revelation is that Jesus is sovereign. He is in control of events and will see us through. If you must suffer persecution, you will do so in Jesus, with Jesus, and for Jesus. We count it joy to share in the sufferings of Christ. We will experience these things in the power and strength of Christ.

Whatever this plague of spiritual darkness may be, if you cling to Jesus, you will triumph over it. It is intended for those who have rejected the gospel.

"The sixth angel sounded his trumpet, and I heard a voice coming from the horns of the golden altar that is before God. It said to the sixth angel who had the trumpet, 'Release the four angels who are bound at the great river Euphrates.' And the four angels who had been kept ready for this very hour and day and month and year were released to kill a third of mankind. The number of the mounted troops was two hundred million. I heard their number" (Revelation 9:13–16). The voice comes from "the horns of the golden altar that is before God." This is a clear reference to the altar of burnt incense that sat in the Holy Place of the tabernacle, just at the entrance to the Most Holy Place. The altar of incense represented the prayers of God's people ascending before the throne. The sixth trumpet is an answer to those prayers. It is specifically an answer to the prayers of those who have been martyred for the sake of the gospel. You remember their cry in Revelation 6:10, "How long, Sovereign Lord, holy and true, until you judge the inhabitants of the earth and avenge our blood?"

The sixth trumpet releases the four angels at the Euphrates. The Euphrates River represents the border between God's people and their enemies; therefore, the enemies of God's people were thought of as coming from beyond Euphrates. The angels that stand guard are ordered to stand aside and allow the enemies of God to have free reign.

To this point, God has restrained the enemies of His people, but those restraints are partially released in the fifth trumpet; in the sixth, they are completely lifted. The description in the sixth trumpet is of a more menacing force than the one found in the fifth.

I believe that contextual evidence suggests that the conflict here is more spiritual than physical. It is a conflict of ideas. This is a spiritual battle instead of a military one. However, during this time there will likely be more martyrs. Men, women, and children will willingly give their lives for the sake of Christ.

John continues, "The rest of mankind that were not killed by these plagues still did not repent of the work of their hands; they did not stop worshiping demons, and idols of gold, silver, bronze, stone and wood—idols that cannot see or hear or walk. Nor did they repent of their murders, their magic arts, their sexual immorality or their thefts" (Revelation 9:20, 21).

There will come a day when the lines are clearly drawn. The choice will be clear to all. Either you are a follower of Jesus Christ, or you are not. At that point, no amount of pleading will change anyone's mind. When the decisions of the inhabitants of earth become this calcified, Christ declares the time has come to end it all.

This is when God will vindicate the blood of the martyrs, thus vindicating His character. Jesus must return and put an end to all sin, sickness, and suffering. It is time for the seventh trumpet, the announcement of the Second Coming.

Chapters 10 and 11 provide an interlude between the sixth and seventh trumpets. One of the scenes we are shown in chapter 11 is the measuring of the temple of God. This is reminiscent of the Old Testament Day of Atonement, a time when God's people were restored to relationship with God. They were sealed as belonging to Him.

The measuring of the temple should be seen in this light as well as in the light of the pause between the sixth and seventh seal—a time given to seal God's people and prepare them for heaven. Measuring the temple is about God's people being sealed in preparation for His return. When they have been sealed, the seventh trumpet blows.

The seventh angel sounded his trumpet, and there were loud voices in heaven, which said:

"The kingdom of the world has become the kingdom of
      our Lord and of his Christ,
   and he will reign for ever and ever."

And the twenty-four elders, who were seated on their thrones before God, fell on their faces and worshiped God, saying:

"We give thanks to you, Lord God Almighty,
   the One who is and who was,
because you have taken your great power
   and have begun to reign.
The nations were angry;
   and your wrath has come.
The time has come for judging the dead,
   and for rewarding your servants the prophets
and your saints and those who reverence your name,
   both small and great—
and for destroying those who destroy the earth"
                                 (Revelation 11:15–18).

The seventh trumpet announces the second coming of Jesus. Heaven celebrates Christ's return as the twenty-four elders and the hosts of heaven worship God. They give thanks to God, "the One who is and who was." God is praised for His righteous judgments against those who have rejected Him, and for the rewards He gives to those who have been faithful to Him.

Destruction awaits the enemies of God. The bullies get their due and we are rescued. Jesus comes to rescue us from the forces of evil. The reign of Christ in the universe is made complete.

No wonder we worship Him: "The kingdom of the world has become the kingdom of our Lord and of his Christ, and he will reign for ever and ever."

While the seven trumpets can paint a rather menacing portrait of events on planet Earth before the return of Jesus, the big picture is that of Christ's sovereignty. All things are in His hands. He alone controls the events on planet Earth, and He alone will see us through those perilous times to the ultimate victory.

No matter how bad the storm, as long as I know that Christ is in control, I can sleep at night.

CHAPTER NINE

The One Who Planned Your Salvation

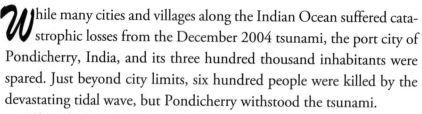

Revelation 12 & 13

*W*hile many cities and villages along the Indian Ocean suffered cata-strophic losses from the December 2004 tsunami, the port city of Pondicherry, India, and its three hundred thousand inhabitants were spared. Just beyond city limits, six hundred people were killed by the devastating tidal wave, but Pondicherry withstood the tsunami.

When the French colonized the city 250 years ago, they built a mas-sive stone seawall. Year after year, the French continued to strengthen the wall, piling huge boulders along its mile-and-a-quarter length.

The French stopped building Pondicherry's seawall in 1957, but their work prepared the city for a disaster five decades later. The city was saved because someone had a plan.

From the beginning of time, God has had a plan. Before the worlds were created, God had a plan. Before Adam and Eve sinned, God had a plan to restore us to peace with Himself.

God has always had a plan.

Revelation reveals God's great plan. While it is certainly a book of mysterious symbols—beasts, dragons, and signs and wonders—those strange symbols help fill in the details of God's plan. The first eleven chapters give us a broad overview of God's workings in the world from the Cross to the Second Coming. The last half of this book now focuses on the events prior to the Second Coming.

But before John takes us there, he provides a review of the history of the world in order to remind us what this was all about in the first place. John tells us that a great struggle has existed between the forces of good and evil. That great cosmic conflict is behind everything we see here on earth, and it is behind every event of your life.

The outcome of the struggle is no longer in doubt. We know that good triumphs over evil, but in the midst of the battle, we sometimes forget this important point.

In chapters 12 and 13 John reminds us of that great conflict and that the outcome has already been determined. "And there was war in heaven. Michael and his angels fought against the dragon, and the dragon and his angels fought back. But he was not strong enough, and they lost their place in heaven. The great dragon was hurled down— that ancient serpent called the devil, or Satan, who leads the whole world astray. He was hurled to the earth, and his angels with him" (Revelation 12:7–9).

John actually presents this passage as sort of a parenthetical statement in the midst of chapter 12. I've chosen to begin with it as a means of preserving the chronology.

Sin began in heaven. Lucifer was a covering cherub, an angel of extreme beauty who was elevated above the other angels. Scripture tells us that pride entered Lucifer's heart and caused him to rebel against God. Lucifer's arguments against God convinced a third of the angels to follow his rebellion, as we will see later when we learn from our study of verse 4 that stars represent angels.

John describes this as war, war that spread to this planet when Lucifer was cast here and tempted Adam and Eve. When they fell, the taint of sin fell on all their progeny. Everyone on this planet now has a natural inclination to sin. Sin separates us from God. This separation results, naturally, in death, since God is the only source of life.

But God had seen this coming and already had a plan. He could not bear the thought of allowing men to perish because of sin.

God's plan was to send a Substitute who could take the penalty of sin upon Himself. That Substitute was to be Jesus, the Second Person of the Godhead. The plan was announced to Adam and Eve, and a system of sacrifices was established to serve as a visible reminder of the price heaven would pay for man's sin.

Finally, when everything was ready, Jesus came to earth as a baby. Chapter 12 tells the story:

> A great and wondrous sign appeared in heaven: a woman clothed with the sun, with the moon under her feet and a crown of twelve stars on her head. She was pregnant and cried out in pain as she was about to give birth. Then another sign appeared in heaven: an enormous red dragon with seven heads and ten horns and seven crowns on his heads. His tail swept a third of the stars out of the sky and flung them to the earth. The dragon stood in front of the woman who was about to give birth, so that he might devour her child the moment it was born. She gave birth to a son, a male child, who will rule all the nations with an iron scepter. And her child was snatched up to God and to his throne. The woman fled into the desert to a place prepared for her by God, where she might be taken care of for 1,260 days (Revelation 12:1–6).

The woman in verse 1 represents the Old Testament church at the time of Jesus' birth. The dragon of verse 3 is Satan as he uses various nations to fulfill his evil intent. The dragon is red, the color of persecution, and he has seven heads, ten horns, and seven crowns. Animals with multiple heads represent nations. The same can be said of horns and crowns.

This clearly tells us that Satan has been allowed to work through various nations throughout history. He has made these nations persecuting powers whose goal it was to inhibit the spread of the gospel or, better yet, to destroy God's people.

At the time of the birth of Jesus, Satan was able to use Rome as he attempted to destroy the Christ child at His birth. That's what John is portraying when he speaks of the dragon standing in front of the woman who was ready to give birth in order that he might devour the Baby. Verse 5 makes it clear that this Baby was Jesus, for He alone "will rule all the nations with an iron scepter."

The last part of verse 5, "And her child was snatched up to God and to his throne," is a picture of the Ascension.

Next, when John speaks of the woman fleeing to the wilderness for 1,260 days, he is referring to how Satan poured out his wrath against the followers of Jesus with special ferocity during the Dark Ages. There was a period of more than twelve centuries during which fifty to eighty million Christians were martyred for their belief in the gospel.

What John is telling us in the first nine verses is that when sin entered this planet, God put His plan into action. He sent Jesus to live, suffer, and die in our place as the sacrifice for our sins; that is, Jesus paid the price for our violation of God's law. Satan realized it was time for Jesus to be born and attempted to destroy Him, using King Herod to have all the children in Bethlehem two years old and younger put to death. An angel warned Joseph through a dream of Herod's intent, and so Joseph and Mary took Jesus to Egypt until the danger had passed.

After the crucifixion of Jesus, Satan turned his wrath against God's people.

Then I heard a loud voice in heaven say:

> "Now have come the salvation and the power and the
> kingdom of our God,
> and the authority of his Christ.
> For the accuser of our brothers,
> who accuses them before our God day and night,
> has been hurled down.
> They overcame him
> by the blood of the Lamb
> and by the word of their testimony;
> they did not love their lives so much
> as to shrink from death" (Revelation 12:10, 11).

The loud voice announces the gospel, God's plan to redeem man. The gospel is the good news of how Jesus has bridged the gap between you and the Father. The gospel is the good news of how Jesus has overcome sin and the devil.

In spite of Satan's attempts throughout the history of the world to persecute and destroy God's people, "salvation and the power and the kingdom of our God, and the authority of his Christ" has come. Jesus has brought salvation to all who will receive Him. He has given us power to overcome the devil and his evil kingdom.

The kingdom of God is now within you, and you have been given the authority of Christ for overcoming the devil. You are not helpless before him—he is helpless before you when you are in Christ.

Occasionally someone comes to me with a concern about demons, who they believe are living in their house. They tell me stories of knocking, of cold presences in the house, and of family members waking up with the feel of an icy, cold hand on their neck. The stories are of demonic harassment.

Whenever I hear these stories, I go to the house and pray in every room there, claiming that room for Jesus as I command that the demons depart. In every case, the demon presence leaves the house and the family tells me that they have no further problems.

The truth is, that family could have done what I did if they had only realized that their position in Christ had given them the power of the kingdom and the authority of Christ. I am not special in that regard. Demons did not leave the house because of me—they left because of Jesus and the power and authority that He gives His children. We have power to overcome the devil.

How do we overcome the devil? Verse 11 says, "They overcame him by the blood of the Lamb and by the word of their testimony."

Jesus' shed blood is all that is necessary to give you complete victory. That blood saves you, gives you the power and the kingdom and the authority of Christ.

Everything depends on the blood of Jesus. His sacrifice is the key.

The blood of Jesus was the key component in God's plan to overcome that great red dragon.

The remainder of the chapter tells how Satan has pursued God's people with persecution and with a flood of false doctrine. There was a time of great persecution that lasted a little over twelve centuries. Scripture expresses that time period in several different ways. In one place this period of persecution is portrayed as 1,260 days, in another as 42 months, and yet another as a time, times, and a half time. All of these expressions refer to the same period of persecution we mentioned earlier, a time when millions willingly gave their lives for Christ and the gospel.

God countered these measures by allowing His people to flee to the "wilderness"; here it was difficult to find them, either to persecute them or to give them false doctrine. During the Dark Ages, the Waldenses and others hid in the mountains and in caves as God preserved a portion of His people from persecution and a flood of false doctrine.

All of this is a part of that great conflict between God and Satan that has been raging since the day Satan's rebellion in heaven, and it will continue until the final destruction of Satan at the end of the age.

When Lucifer fell from heaven, he declared,

> "I will ascend to heaven;
> I will raise my throne
>   above the stars of God;
> I will sit enthroned on the mount of assembly,
>   on the utmost heights of the sacred mountain.
> I will ascend above the tops of the clouds;
>   I will make myself like the Most High" (Isaiah 14:13, 14).

It has been Satan's desire to usurp the worship of God's people. He longs to take God's place and become the object of worship.

John illustrates this by referring to Satan's counterfeit trinity. Chapter 12 introduces a red dragon that represents Satan as he works through various kingdoms and powers. In chapter 13 we see the dragon again, but now two more beasts are presented.

And the dragon stood on the shore of the sea.

And I saw a beast coming out of the sea. He had ten horns and seven heads, with ten crowns on his horns, and on each head a blasphemous name. The beast I saw resembled a leopard, but had feet like those of a bear and a mouth like that of a lion. The dragon gave the beast his power and his throne and great authority. One of the heads of the beast seemed to have had a fatal wound, but the fatal wound had been healed. The whole world was astonished and followed the beast. Men worshiped the dragon because he had given authority to the beast, and they also worshiped the beast and asked, "Who is like the beast? Who can make war against him?" (Revelation 13:1–4).

Satan, the dragon, calls a beast from the sea. This beast has—or uses—kings and kingdoms, as evidenced by the fact that he has multiple heads and also has horns and crowns. This beast is the successor of all the beasts that have come before him, and it arises sometime after the breakup of the Roman Empire.

There is something else about this beast, however. This beast speaks blasphemy.

Blasphemy is the act of claiming equality with God, or of claiming prerogatives of God alone. In addition, this beast receives its power and authority from the great red dragon, which we have already learned represents Satan.

It is interesting to note that while on earth, Jesus was given authority from God the Father. This beast that was summoned from the sea by the dragon received its power and authority from the dragon.

One of the heads of this beast was wounded with a deadly wound, but the head was healed. Jesus received a deadly wound but was raised to life. This beast is a counterfeit Jesus and demands the worship of the people.

There is more here about this beast. "The beast was given a mouth to utter proud words and blasphemies and to exercise his authority for forty-two months. He opened his mouth to blaspheme God, and to slander his name and his dwelling place and those who live in heaven" (Revelation 13:5, 6).

In Daniel 7, the little horn had a mouth that spoke blasphemies. The time given to the beast from the sea to exercise control was forty-two months, the same length of time that the little horn of Daniel exercised power. All of this points to a religio-political power that played a role in persecuting God's people for about a twelve-hundred-year period beginning during the Dark Ages. Martin Luther and other Reformers identified the little horn of Daniel 7 and the beast from the sea in Revelation 13 as representing the papacy. Others, such as William G. Johnsson, point to any power that coerces matters of faith as being a "little-horn" power or a "beast" power.

Satan is involved in a great war with God—a war that began with rebellion in heaven. When Satan is not able to touch God, he goes after God's people. When Jesus was on the earth, Satan had opportunity to take his best shots at God Himself. After the death, resurrection, and ascension of Jesus, Satan went back to work on the people of God.

This beast from the sea pours out Satan's intense hatred for God and His people. Satan is intensely jealous of Jesus, and his desire is to be worshiped as Jesus is worshiped. Satan longs to replace the Godhead.

John says of this blasphemous beast from the sea: "All inhabitants of the earth will worship the beast—all whose names have not been written in the book of life belonging to the Lamb that was slain from the creation of the world" (Revelation 13:8).

If we refuse to worship the beast, we belong to Jesus. Our names are written in the Lamb's book of life. Your name was written there when you asked Jesus to be your Savior. That means that your salvation is sealed in Christ Jesus as long as you remain faithful to Him. Satan hates you because you are sealed by God and worship Him alone.

So far we have the red dragon and the beast from the sea, but the final third of the substitute trinity appears in verse 11.

> Then I saw another beast, coming out of the earth. He had two horns like a lamb, but he spoke like a dragon. He exercised all the authority of the first beast on his behalf, and made the earth and its inhabitants worship the first beast, whose fatal wound had been healed. And he performed great and miraculous signs, even causing fire to come down from heaven to earth in full view of men. Because of the signs he was given power to do on behalf of the first beast, he deceived the inhabitants of the earth. He ordered them to set up an image in honor of the beast who was wounded by the sword and yet lived (Revelation 13:11–14).

The earlier beast came from the sea, while this beast comes from the earth. Together they signify the worldwide scope of Satan's activities.

This beast, on the surface, appears to be friendly. When he speaks, however, his evil nature becomes evident. This lamblike beast speaks for the dragon and receives his authority from the dragon. He is Satan's pawn.

This beast attempts to force everyone to worship the beast whose deadly wound had been healed. Again we see coercion as the means by which these beast powers attempt to receive the worship that is due to God alone.

If the red dragon represents the counterfeit God the Father, and the sea beast with the deadly wound represents the counterfeit Jesus, then this last beast is the counterfeit Holy Spirit. This power seemingly works miracles in an effort to get the whole world to worship the beast whose wound had been healed. The land beast attempts to coerce people to worship the sea beast.

> He was given power to give breath to the image of the first beast, so that it could speak and cause all who refused to worship the image to be killed. He also forced everyone, small and great, rich and poor, free and slave, to receive a mark on his right hand or on his forehead, so that no one could buy or sell

unless he had the mark, which is the name of the beast or the number of his name.

This calls for wisdom. If anyone has insight, let him calculate the number of the beast, for it is man's number. His number is 666 (Revelation 13:15–18).

In a sense, this beast represents any power that attempts to force or coerce matters of worship and conscience. Just as God seals or marks His people, so too does the substitute trinity mark its worshipers.

Those who do not have the beast's mark will be unable to buy or sell. Economic coercion is now added to the weapons of persecution and martyrdom in Satan's effort to force people to change allegiance and to worship the beast instead of Christ.

In verse 18, we are told that the beast has a number—666. Many have attempted to identify a person or a power as the beast power by using Roman numerals taken from a name or insignia and adding them up to make the number 666. This practice has no biblical precedence and is probably not helpful since this number is more spiritual than literal.

Attempts have been made to tie this number directly to the pope by claiming that the papal title, *Vicarius Fillii Dei*, was found on a papal miter and that when the numeric value of the Roman numerals contained in that title were added together they added up to the number 666. There are numerous problems with this, however, and we should be careful how we use it.

First, there is no documented evidence that *Vicarius Fillii Dei* has ever appeared on a papal tiara or miter. Second, there is no evidence that this title has ever been applied to the pope. Its only documented application is found in a document, *The Donation of Constantine*, that is a known forgery, and even there, the title is only applied to Peter and not to the pope.

Another problem has to do with the language required to make this happen. Latin was a language in little use during the days of John the revelator. The entire world spoke Greek. In order to make the supposed papal title add up to the number 666, you must use Roman numerals, and even then, you must be selective about which language and which alphabet you use when attempting to make the computations.

The thirteenth chapter of Revelation provides plenty of information to assist us in identifying the beast. That, however, is not my purpose here. (Many others have covered this elsewhere.) It is my hope to understand this number from a more spiritual perspective.

Six is the number of humanity, the number of incompletion or imperfection. Seven is the number of perfection. Since 666 is the number of a man, it represents something human, something that falls short of divine perfection.

Three sixes seems to point to the substitute trinity as opposed to the three sevens, the divine Trinity. The number 666 symbolizes the counterfeit trinity that attempts to force the world to worship the beast in place of Jesus. I have borrowed the term *counterfeit trinity* from a commentary on Revelation by Ranko Stefanovic, entitled *Revelation of Jesus Christ*.

The issue in the final crisis will be worship. Satan has long desired the worship of the universe. The desire of the three beasts is that you worship the beast which had a deadly wound that was healed. But God says that He alone is to be worshiped. Our allegiance and our worship belong to Him alone.

Those who do not receive God's seal will be vulnerable to the deceptions of the substitute trinity and will worship them instead of the God of heaven. However, those who trust in Jesus—those who have been sealed by God—are protected from this end-time deception. Although all of this sounds confusing and ominous, remember that this is being shared to help us see God's plan. Do not fear. God has always had a plan for your salvation. That plan is based on the blood of Jesus, and through that blood you have the power of Christ on your side.

God has a plan to combat the forces of evil. He has a plan to rescue us from the red dragon, the sea beast, and the beast whose wound was healed.

We learn about these three creatures in order to better understand Satan's plan. When we know what the enemy is up to, we are better equipped to combat his strategy.

Ultimately, the thing we need to know is that God's plan is foolproof! He has already won the victory over the counterfeit trinity.

Chapter 12 has already told us how we will win this battle.

Then I heard a loud voice in heaven say:

> "Now have come the salvation and the power and the
> kingdom of our God,
>   and the authority of his Christ.
> For the accuser of our brothers,
>   who accuses them before our God day and night,
>   has been hurled down.
> They overcame him
>   by the blood of the Lamb
>   and by the word of their testimony;
> they did not love their lives so much
>   as to shrink from death" (Revelation 12:10, 11).

The choice is clear. Either you worship God or you worship Satan's counterfeit.

You have nothing to fear from these beasts if you hold to the blood of the Lamb. Live in Jesus today. That is the way to be ready for the last great deception, for as we live daily in Christ Jesus, He seals us and thus protects us from the devil.

We overcome by the blood of the Lamb. This is God's great plan. When I know God's plan and realize that He assures me that His plan will work itself out according to His will, my fearful heart is put at ease. I can rest in full assurance that God is in control. As long as I trust in Him, I need not fear.

Jesus is like Pondicherry's seawall; He protects all who remain within Him.

CHAPTER TEN

The One Who Rescues You

Revelation 14

Revelation 12 and 13 have given us a bird's eye view of the history of the great controversy between Christ and Satan. It warns of a counterfeit trinity that attempts to force people to worship it, as opposed to the true Trinity, the Father, Son, and Holy Spirit.

That's the big picture of the conflict.

Now Revelation 14 contains God's response to Satan's work. God responds first by spreading truth abroad and helping the world realize the central focus of the issues that face the earth.

The last great issue will be over worship, and God's people will call the world to worship the Creator God.

> Then I looked, and there before me was the Lamb, standing on Mount Zion, and with him 144,000 who had his name and his Father's name written on their foreheads. And I heard a sound from heaven like the roar of rushing waters and like a loud peal of thunder. The sound I heard was like that of harpists playing their harps. And they sang a new song before the throne and before the four living creatures and the elders. No one could learn the song except the 144,000 who had been redeemed from the earth. These are those who did not defile themselves with women, for they kept themselves pure. They

follow the Lamb wherever he goes. They were purchased from among men and offered as firstfruits to God and the Lamb. No lie was found in their mouths; they are blameless (Revelation 14:1–5).

In verse 1 we see the Lamb, which is Jesus, our Sacrifice. He is standing on Mount Zion. Because in the Old Testament, Mount Zion is seen as the center of God's government on earth, we know that Jesus is here seen as the King of this earth.

Around Jesus we see the 144,000. This is a symbolic number and not the exact number of those who will be saved. It symbolizes the church. The church is God's great spiritual army as it battles against Satan and his army. The 144,000 represents the church, which is fully devoted to God with a pure faith as it prepares to battle the forces of darkness.

John hears this group singing a song of the redeemed. The 144,000 prepare for battle by worshiping the Lamb. They sing a song of redemption as they worship Jesus, our Redeemer.

Verse 4 says they "did not defile themselves with women." The Bible speaks of rebellion against God as adultery. The false church is symbolized as an impure woman. Those who turn from the true God commit fornication with this woman. Those who stand with God remain faithful to their Husband, God. They have decided that they will worship the true God alone, and will remain faithful to Him.

The fact that the 144,000 are said to be "blameless" does not mean that they have never committed sin. Their sins have been forgiven; the blood of the Lamb covers them. They have not arrived at some perfected state but are viewed by God as perfect because they share in the perfection of Christ through the gift of His grace.

The last great battle is more of a spiritual battle; thus, the implements of warfare are not automatic weapons, tanks, battleships, or smart bombs. The implements of warfare are spiritual truths.

To bring this conflict to a close, Jesus gives a message for His army to carry to the world. This is a message of rescue and warning. It is God's last message before His glorious return.

"Then I saw another angel flying in midair, and he had the eternal gospel to proclaim to those who live on the earth—to every nation, tribe, language and people. He said in a loud voice, 'Fear God and give him glory, because the hour of his judgment has come. Worship him who made the heavens, the earth, the sea and the springs of water' " (Revelation 14:6, 7).

Three angels are seen in chapter 14, each with a portion of a three-part warning message. These angels carry messages that help prepare earth's inhabitants for the last great conflict. The angels carry messages that are to be delivered by God's people on earth.

The first angel has the "eternal gospel to proclaim to those who live on the earth." The gospel is the good news about Jesus' sacrifice for us.

I have heard the term *gospel* used to describe the whole of Christian teaching—an entire slate of doctrines. As important as these might be, the "gospel" is more restrictive in its meaning. The gospel refers to the plan of salvation—Christ's substitutionary death on Calvary, His promise of forgiveness and eternal life for all who by faith receive the merits of that death, and the promised rescue from this planet through the Second Coming. That is the gospel, and that is the primary message that God has given to a dying planet. It is a message of rescue.

That message begins with knowledge of who we are. We are sinners. "For all have sinned and fall short of the glory of God" (Romans 3:23). As sinners, we deserve the most severe of punishments. "For the wages of sin is death" (Romans 6:23). As sinners deserving death, we can do nothing to save ourselves. No amount of effort on our part will secure our salvation. "For it is by grace you have been saved, through faith—and this not from yourselves, it is the gift of God—not by works, so that no one can boast" (Ephesians 2:8, 9).

But God loves us too much to allow our sins to separate us from

Himself. He longed for us to be reconciled to Hims‹
strated that love through Jesus. "God demonstrates h
us in this: While we were still sinners, Christ died f‹
5:8). "For God so loved the world that he gave his on‹
that whoever believes in him shall not perish but have eternal life"
(John 3:16).

How does this help us? How do we access the merits of Christ's
death for our salvation?

"That if you confess with your mouth, 'Jesus is Lord,' and believe
in your heart that God raised him from the dead, you will be saved.
For it is with your heart that you believe and are justified, and it is
with your mouth that you confess and are saved. As the Scripture says,
'Anyone who trusts in him will never be put to shame' " (Romans
10:9–11).

The promise to save us is culminated by the return of Jesus to take
His children home. This will be the crowning act of the gospel. " 'Do
not let your hearts be troubled. Trust in God; trust also in me. In my
Father's house are many rooms; if it were not so, I would have told
you. I am going there to prepare a place for you. And if I go and prepare a place for you, I will come back and take you to be with me that
you also may be where I am' " (John 14:1–3).

This is the gospel. If you have never received the gospel, make to-
day the day that you do. Come to Jesus, confessing your need of Him.
Accept the gift of His sacrifice for your sins, and claim salvation today.
It really is that simple!

This is the heart of God's last warning message for the world. Jesus
died for sinners and provided a means for their escape from death.
The gospel is the promise of eternal life with Jesus.

The first angel's message continues in verse 7. " 'Fear God and give
him glory, because the hour of his judgment has come. Worship him
who made the heavens, the earth, the sea and the springs of water' "
(Revelation 14:7).

The command is to "fear God and give him glory" and to "worship
him." Remember that the last great issue will be the issue of worship.

e question is, Will you worship the God of heaven or the counterfeit trinity?

The word *fear* means, "to be struck with amazement, to be afraid of one, or to reverence, venerate, and treat with deference or reverential obedience." To fear God denotes a relationship with God and a full surrender to His will. God is not to be taken lightly.

We often think of "gentle Jesus, meek and mild." Although this is true, we must also remember that He is called "the Lion of the tribe of Judah."

Do not attempt to declaw or defang this Lion! He is every bit a Lion, and He is to be feared. He is to be reverenced. We are to give glory to God. This is a major element of God's last-day warning message. The message includes a call to worship the Creator God of the universe. Again we come to worship.

Remember the pattern we've seen in Revelation. Every crisis on earth is answered by a worship service in heaven. The angels sing, " 'Holy, holy, holy, Lord God Almighty!' " and " 'Worthy is the Lamb that was slain.' " God's last warning message to planet Earth begins with the gospel and continues with worship.

If you will live in the assurance of eternal life today, and worship God every day, you will be making preparations for the final conflict on planet Earth. That's what we do to prepare for the end of Earth's history. Those who would endure Earth's last cataclysmic events at the end of time will accept the gospel, worship the true God, and live in Christ Jesus every day. That is the message of the first angel of Revelation 14.

But this is only the first part of God's last message to a dying planet—a message of warning and of rescue. His message continues with the second angel in verse 8, but remember that the warnings contained in the messages of the next two angels do not apply to those who have accepted Jesus as Savior and have the seal of God. "A second angel followed and said, 'Fallen! Fallen is Babylon the Great, which made all the nations drink the maddening wine of her adulteries' " (Revelation 14:8). This is a message of warning.

In the Old Testament, Babylon is a religious and political power that opposes God and oppresses His people. That term now appears in Revelation for the first time. Babylon, in Revelation 17, is described as a prostitute woman sitting on "many waters" and the beast. This tells us that Babylon represents an end-time religious alliance made up of that satanic trinity revealed in Revelation 12 and 13.

Babylon, among other things, means "confusion." It is Babylon's goal to confuse the inhabitants of the earth with false doctrine. Babylon is a blasphemous power, exalting itself above God, attempting to take the place of God.

William Johnson writes that Babylon "represents all human attempts to provide the way of salvation, all those plans and programs that, because they are built alone on human reason and devises, attempt to frustrate the divine plan for the world."

This religious alliance will collapse prior to the return of Jesus. While the text makes it sound as if Babylon has already fallen, this is simply a common technique of the prophets. So certain that the thing they've predicted will happen, they speak of it as though it already has. Babylon, the false religious system of the counterfeit trinity, *will fall.*

John said that Babylon "made all the nations drink the maddening wine of her adulteries." In Revelation 17, John shows Babylon as a prostitute woman who makes men drunk with the wine of her fornication.

Throughout Scripture, rebellion against God is spoken of as adultery or as drunkenness. Sexual sin and drunkenness represent open rebellion against God and His kingdom. Babylon, this religious alliance of the counterfeit trinity, attempts to spread her licentious rebellion against God to all the earth.

The message of the second angel is simply a warning against going along with Babylon for the false sense of security it may bring.

We are to take a stand for God. God's end-time people will be characterized by their unwavering loyalty to God, and their faithful obedience to Him.

Babylon is temporary; it will fall. Thus, there is no security there. In contrast, God is permanent; He will never fall. We are, therefore, secure in Him.

There is one more angel with a message, but again, this warning applies only to those who have not received the gospel and, therefore, do not have the seal of God.

> A third angel followed them and said in a loud voice: "If anyone worships the beast and his image and receives his mark on the forehead or on the hand, he, too, will drink of the wine of God's fury, which has been poured full strength into the cup of his wrath. He will be tormented with burning sulfur in the presence of the holy angels and of the Lamb. And the smoke of their torment rises for ever and ever. There is no rest day or night for those who worship the beast and his image, or for anyone who receives the mark of his name" (Revelation 14:9–11).

This message builds on the second angel's message. It says that those who reject the message of the first angel and choose to worship the beast and to receive his mark will receive God's wrath. The angel warns against receiving a mark on the forehead or hand.

The word for "mark" implies a stamp, or an imprinted mark. It was used as a technical term for the imperial stamp on commercial documents or the royal impression on Roman coins. It was also the word used for branding animals and thus denotes ownership. Those who worship the beast receive his mark of ownership.

The mark is given in either the hand or in the forehead. Those who receive the mark in the hand may not actually believe the things the beast stands for. In fact, they may actually believe God to be true and right but, for the sake of convenience, go along with the requirements of the beast. They do not believe in the beast; they comply for the sake of economic or political security. What a tragic mistake!

Those who receive the mark in the forehead actually buy into the things the beast teaches. They have been deceived by his false teachings.

The followers of God receive His seal, or His mark of ownership, in their foreheads. This seal is based on belief. Their minds belong to God. If your mind belongs to God, your body and your behavior naturally follow.

Those who receive the beast's mark are said to " 'drink of the wine of God's fury, which has been poured full strength into the cup of his wrath' " (Revelation 14:10).

In the Old Testament, those who receive God's wrath are depicted as drinking wine from the Lord's cup. While those who receive the seal of God will be rewarded with eternal life, those who receive the beast's mark will receive God's wrath. They have chosen to worship someone other than God, and worship is the last great issue.

This wrath is poured full strength, undiluted, into God's cup. In ancient times wine was often mixed with spices and herbs in order to strengthen its potency. At other times wine was diluted with water in order to weaken it. The wine of God's fury here is poured out without being diluted. Those who have rejected God's call to worship Him alone will receive God's fury without dilution. " 'And the smoke of their torment rises for ever and ever' " (Revelation 14:11).

Having looked at this passage, many have drawn the conclusion that hell will burn forever, yet this same wording is used in the Old Testament when God rained fire and sulfur on Sodom and Gomorrah. Jude tells us that these two cities experience "the punishment of eternal fire" (Jude 7). Of course, Sodom and Gomorrah are not burning today. Our best guess is that the site of Sodom and Gomorrah is now covered by the Dead Sea. At the bottom of that sea are two great tar pits. They are not burning; after all—they are under water! However, God's rain of fire and sulfur had an eternal effect, because the cities were never rebuilt.

Isaiah prophesied that God would punish Edom night and day. Again, it would burn with an unquenchable fire and its smoke would rise up for ever. This simply means that the results of the fire would never be reversed. It would not be quenched until its work was done, and its effects would last forever.

Neither the ancient cities of Sodom and Gomorrah nor Edom are still burning today. However, the effects of God's judgment of fire on those places have been irreversible.

The same is true of the fires of hell. They will not be quenched until their work is done; hence, they are unquenchable.

The fires of hell will be everlasting in that their effects will be everlasting. Sin and sinners will never exist again. The fires of hell will not last forever; their work of destruction, however, will.

Revelation 14 contains three messages for the earth's last days. The messages are of rescue and of warning. These messages are to prepare us for the final conflict.

The first message is a message of the gospel and a call to worship the Creator. This is ultimately a message of rescue. The means of rescue is clearly spelled out. If we would be rescued, we will receive the gospel and worship God exclusively.

The second message is only for those who have not accepted the gospel and is a warning that Babylon, the false trinity's illegitimate system of worship, will one day fall. Babylon is a man-made religion that promotes man-made methods and systems of salvation. They will fail and Babylon will fall. There is no security there.

And finally, the third message is a warning of the punishment that will befall those who reject the call to worship the true God and worship the beast instead. Again, this warning is not for those who have received the gospel and remain true to God. Those who reject the gospel receive a mark, and by receiving his mark, they are marking themselves for eternal annihilation. They will be the recipients of God's wrath.

But God does not end His warning messages with this negative note. Instead, He identifies those who bear His seal. "This calls for patient endurance on the part of the saints who obey God's commandments and remain faithful to Jesus" (Revelation 14:12). God's last-day people will be obedient to God. They will keep His commandments, because they have faith in Jesus. These people have been sealed as belonging to God alone. They are the ones who await the return of Jesus.

The rest of the chapter speaks of a harvest. This means that now that the last messages have been delivered, it is time for judgment to be poured out on God's enemies and the enemies of His people. But I want to focus just a bit longer on the three angels of Revelation 14. Their messages all center on just a few ideas.

The three angels begin with a proclamation of the gospel; they make clear that the last great issue centers around worship. God's wrath is reserved for those who reject the gospel and worship anything other than God alone. God will rescue those who have faith in Jesus and are obedient to Him.

I urge you today, claim God's sealing on your life. Receive the gift of salvation won for you by Christ's sacrifice. Reserve your worship for God alone, for only He is worthy.

In return, God has promised to preserve you in the last day, and to rescue you from a dying planet.

CHAPTER ELEVEN

The One Who Forgives You

Revelation 14

Revelation 14 has such an important message we need to give it a deeper look. Of particular interest to me are verses 6 and 7, which have brought me considerable comfort during turbulent times of my life.

Dr. John Duncan taught Hebrew in Edinburgh long ago. John was sitting in a church during Communion. He was feeling so personally unworthy that, when the elements came around, John allowed the bread and wine to pass. As John was sitting there, he noticed a girl in the congregation who, when the bread and wine came around, also allowed them to pass, and then broke down into tears. That sight brought back to the old saint the truth that he had forgotten. And in a whisper that carried across the church he said, "Take it, lassie, take it. It's meant for sinners."

Then Dr. John Duncan partook of those emblems himself.

The broken body and shed blood of Christ was meant for you, a sinner. That is the message of Christianity. The message preached by Peter, Paul, John, and the others was this: "Your sins can be forgiven and you can live forever, all because of the sacrifice of Jesus. You cannot save yourself. No amount of good works will ever make you good enough for heaven. Only faith in Jesus can do that. Confess your sins; trust in Jesus, and He will save you."

This, in essence, is the gospel! It was the message preached by the apostles. It was the theme of the early church. As that message was proclaimed, Christianity spread throughout the world!

Revelation tells us that it is still the message God has for our planet in earth's last hours. It is a message born by angels to bring comfort to troubled hearts: "Then I saw another angel flying in midair, and he had the eternal gospel to proclaim to those who live on the earth—to every nation, tribe, language and people. He said in a loud voice, 'Fear God and give him glory, because the hour of his judgment has come. Worship him who made the heavens, the earth, the sea and the springs of water' " (Revelation 14:6, 7).

I love the fact that when God sent a message for today, the very first thing He mentioned was the gospel. The angel carried the "eternal gospel." What is the eternal gospel? *Evangelion* (which we call gospel) is a Greek word that signifies good, merry, glad, and joyful tidings, that makes a man's heart glad, and makes him sing, dance, and leap for joy. The gospel is neither a discussion nor a debate. It is an announcement.

Islam is centered in a sacred city, Mecca, where there is a sacred building, the Kaaba. In this building is a sacred stone that, they say, came down from heaven. This is probably true, for the stone is most likely a meteorite.

Christians believe it was not a stone that came down from heaven but a message, a word, a gospel! Christ died to save sinners! The eternal gospel is the message that was proclaimed by the church of the first century.

In his 1942 devotional book *Abundant Living*, E. Stanley Jones, Methodist doctor and missionary to India, writes, "The early Christians did not say in dismay: 'Look what the world has come to,' but in delight, 'Look what has come to the world.' They saw not merely the ruin, but the Resource for the reconstruction of that ruin. They saw not merely that sin did abound, but that grace did much more abound. On that assurance the pivot of history swung from blank despair, loss of moral nerve, and fatalism, to faith and confidence that at last sin had met its match."

Early Christians understood and accepted the eternal gospel. Their acceptance of this message changed their lives and, subsequently, the world. That same message is the message that the church of today most needs. It proclaims to us, "Look what has come to the world! Sin has met its match!"

If we could be saved through human kindness or clear thinking, Jesus either would have formed a sensitivity group and urged us to share our feelings, or He would have founded a school and asked us to have discussions. But knowing the ways of God, the way of the world, and the persistence of human sin, He took up the cross, called disciples, gathered the church, and bade us follow Him down a different path of freedom.

Ours is a message that saves. Christ died for sinners.

You didn't do anything to become a sinner. Someone else did that for you. "For just as through the disobedience of the one man the many were made sinners, so also through the obedience of the one man the many will be made righteous" (Romans 5:19).

It was the disobedience of Adam that determined that you would be born with a natural tendency to sin.

A pastor was teaching a Bible class to a group of students when he asked a question of a young boy. "Now, Billy, tell me what we must do before we can expect to be forgiven for our sins."

Without hesitation, Billy replied, "First we gotta sin."

Billy was right. Sinning comes naturally to all of us. We were born as natural sinners because of the decision of our first parents, Adam and Eve. John Newton said, "I remember two things: that I am a great sinner and that Christ is a great Savior."

You didn't do anything to become a sinner. Someone else did that for you. Just the same, you can't do anything to save yourself. Someone else must do that as well.

The last part of that passage in Romans 5 reads, "so also by one Man's obedience many will be made righteous" (verse 19, NKJV).

You didn't do anything to become a sinner, and you can't do anything to be made righteous. Only Jesus, the perfect Man, can make you righteous. Only by faith in Jesus can you be saved. "For it is by grace you have been saved, through faith—and this not from yourselves; it is the gift of God—not by works, so that no one can boast" (Ephesians 2:8, 9). We are saved through faith in the grace of God.

The eternal gospel is the truth that everyone can be saved if they will call upon Jesus. We must believe that He is God in the flesh—that He bled and died for our sins, and then was raised to life and ascended unto the Father.

I believe it was Marva Dawn who noted that the Hebrew evening/morning sequence conditions us to the rhythms of grace. You remember the Creation story in Genesis, don't you? "And the evening and the morning was the first day."

We go to sleep, and God begins His work. We wake into a world we didn't make, and into a salvation we didn't earn.

Jesus paid your penalty. Jesus forgives your sins. Jesus gives you the gift of eternal life. This is the first part of the message carried by the angel.

There are only two kinds of religion in the world. You can list every "ism," every cult, every religion in the world under one category. They all say, "Do, do, do." Only Christianity says, "Done." Christ has done it all. That is the gospel!

The gospel is not so much a demand as it is an offer, an offer of new life to man by the grace of God.

Blaise Pascal, when he understood the gospel, wrote, "The gospel to me is simply irresistible." I must agree with Pascal. When I began to understand the gospel, it became simply irresistible!

The angel's message continues in verse 7. " 'Fear God and give him glory, because the hour of his judgment has come. Worship him who made the heavens, the earth, the sea and the springs of water' " (Revelation 14:7).

First and foremost, the angel tells us that we are to receive the gospel. Christ died for sinners. But, secondly, the angel declares that a day of judgment is at hand. God will not allow this world to continue as it is indefinitely. A day is coming when He will call all things into account.

On that day, who will be found worthy? Only those who believe the gospel! Only those who trust in Christ, those who trust in the blood of the Lamb, will stand in the day of judgment. In fact, for those who trust Christ, judgment is a wonderful thing because through judgment we find vindication. Our lives are covered with the blood of Jesus, so when the accuser points the finger at us, God says, "I find no fault in him; I find no fault in her." We are covered with the robe of Christ's righteousness and God sees nothing amiss. Our lives are vindicated, and we are assured of heaven. That is good news indeed!

But for those who do not trust in Christ, judgment is frightening. If you have to stand by yourself in judgment, you are liable to receive justice, not grace.

No one wants justice in the day of God's judgment. We all want grace and we all need grace! Grace is given only to those who claim it through faith in Jesus. All others stand alone on that day, and therefore, they get justice. Justice will be their ruin because they all, like us, are sinners.

Why would you choose justice over grace? It doesn't make sense. That's why the gospel is such incredibly good news. God grants grace to those who give their lives to God.

Grace is a very rare thing. We don't find much of it in the world. The world gives justice, not grace.

Lillie Baltrip is a good bus driver. In fact, according to the Fort Worth *Star-Telegram* of June 17, 1988, the Houston school district nominated her for a safe-driving award. Her colleagues even trusted her to drive a busload of them to an awards ceremony for safe drivers. Unfortunately, on the way to the ceremony, Lillie turned a corner too sharply and flipped the bus, sending herself and sixteen others to the hospital for minor emergency treatment. Did Lillie, accident free for the whole year, get her award anyway? No! Award committees rarely operate on the principle of grace. Lillie did not get the award.

How fortunate we are that even when we don't maintain a spotless life-record, our final reward depends on God's grace, not on our performance!

The angel proclaimed the everlasting gospel, and he warned of the day of judgment. However, contained in the angel's warning message is a solution to the problem of judgment. In the last half of verse 7, the angel encourages us to " 'worship Him who made heaven and earth, the sea and springs of water' " (Revelation 14:7).

Again we see that heaven's solution to any problem appears to be worship!

Do you feel uncertain about the future? The answer is to worship God.

Are you weak in your faith? The solution is to worship!

Have you lost your first love, or are you fearful of the day of judgment? Again, the solution is to worship God.

How are we to worship Him? We are to engage in a worship that acknowledges that God is the Creator God of the universe! He made " 'heaven and earth, the sea and springs of water.' " God is worthy of your praise and worship because He is your Creator and your Redeemer.

This is the answer to your problems. You must worship God. You need to worship Him. You were made for the purpose of worshiping God. You will never be whole, never be fulfilled, until you discover your fulfillment, your ultimate purpose, in the worship of God as Creator and Redeemer.

This is the angel's message. It is the message of the everlasting gospel. Christ died to save sinners! It is the message of a day of judgment—a day of vindication and grace for those who trust Christ, and a day of justice and ruin for those who do not.

Not only are we to receive this message, but we are to share it as well. Preachers and evangelists are not the only ones who bear this responsibility. This is the job of the church as a whole, of every member. Your life should speak to these three ingredients of the message of the church today.

I do not mean to imply that you should attempt to force this message down anyone's throat. We are to proclaim the message the same way the members of the church of the first century proclaimed it. We are to live it! *Proclaim by Living It!*

There are two things to do about the gospel—believe it and behave it. Our lives should proclaim the gospel with and without words.

I saw a poster that said, "Preach the gospel. If necessary, use words." That says it all. We are speaking of a lifestyle of evangelism. Our very lives should preach the gospel.

The gospel is not made to dominate the world. It's the grain of sand that upsets the world's machinery. One can't inhale its fragrance and be content to leave everything the way it is.

Evangelism is a lifestyle of proclaiming the gospel by living the gospel every day. Evangelism is having a burden for the souls of men and women and accepting the responsibility for their souls ourselves.

For far too long the church has viewed evangelism as an "event" which was to be conducted by a "professional." That is the fastest way I know to kill a church. If everyone sits around and waits for the professionals to do the work, we are in a lot of trouble.

The gospel is to be proclaimed by the church, and you are the church. Your life must preach to all who see you live. Eventually, as we live the gospel in full view of others, opportunities will arise when it would be appropriate to speak a word about our faith in Christ.

Allow me to be even more forward. Are there people in your life today who you know could benefit from the gospel, but you have not spoken to them of Christ for fear of rejection? Do you have a burden for where your friends, neighbors, and relatives will spend eternity? Are you telling others about what Christ has done for you?

In his autobiography, *Just as I Am*, Billy Graham tells about a conversation he had with John F. Kennedy shortly after Kennedy's election:

> On the way back to the Kennedy house, the president-elect stopped the car and turned to me. "Do you believe in the second coming of Jesus Christ?" he asked.

"I most certainly do."

"Well, does my church believe it?"

"They have it in their creeds."

"They don't preach it," he said. "They don't tell us much about it. I'd like to know what you think."

I explained what the Bible said about Christ coming the first time, dying on the Cross, rising from the dead, and then promising that he would come back again. "Only then," I said, "are we going to have permanent world peace."

"Very interesting," he said, looking away. "We'll have to talk more about that someday." And he drove on.

Several years later, the two met again, at the 1963 National Prayer Breakfast. "I had the flu," Graham remembers. "After I gave my short talk, and he gave his, we walked out of the hotel to his car together, as was always our custom. At the curb, he turned to me. 'Billy, could you ride back to the White House with me? I'd like to see you for a minute.' 'Mr. President, I've got a fever,' I protested. 'Not only am I weak, but I don't want to give you this thing. Couldn't we wait and talk some other time?' It was a cold, snowy day, and I was freezing as I stood there without my overcoat. 'Of course,' he said graciously."

The two men would never meet again. Later that year, Kennedy was shot dead. Graham comments, "His hesitation at the car door, and his request, haunt me still. What was on his mind? Should I have gone with him? It was an irrecoverable moment."

Have you experienced irrecoverable moments with people you know and love? I have.

As a young pastor, one of my members suffered a heart attack. I knew and loved this man. When I walked into the ICU, he was sitting up and doing much better. I attempted to encourage him by saying, "Oh, you'll be out of here in no time."

There was a look of fear in the man's eyes as he responded, "I don't know, pastor. I certainly hope so."

I was uncomfortable with the moment, and so I backed away. I failed to speak to him of his salvation; I failed to press the issue of his confidence in Christ. I brushed it off and said, "Of course you'll get out of here."

Three hours later, that same man had another heart attack and died.

How I wish I had taken the opportunity to speak to him of confidence in Jesus. How I wish I had taken the time to speak to him of his soul. It was an irrecoverable moment. I have made a promise to myself. I never leave a critically ill patient without speaking to them of their soul.

But in reality, we are all critically ill. We are all dying, and all assured of an eternal death and separation from God if we are not connected to the grace of Christ. So why wouldn't we all make a promise to ourselves and to our God never to miss an opportunity to speak to someone about his soul? Why wouldn't we make the promise to live our lives in such a way that others will be drawn to our Savior?

We have such a wonderful treasure in the gospel! What is it that prevents us from sharing it? Why do we tend to hoard it instead of proclaiming it?

Luigi Tarisio was found dead one morning with scarcely a comfort in his home. But when they went through his house they found 246 exquisite violins crammed into an attic. He had been collecting them all his life. The best violin was in the bottom drawer of an old rickety bureau.

In his very devotion to the violin, he had robbed the world of all the music that could have been played on the violins that he had treasured for himself, so that when the greatest of his collection, a Stradivarius, was first played, it had had 147 speechless years until then.

How many of Christ's people are like old Tarisio? In our very love of the church we fail to give the glad tidings to the world; in our zeal for the truth we forget to publish it.

When will we all learn that the good news needs not just to be cherished, but needs to be told? All people need to hear it. That Jesus died to save sinners is not only the good news—it is the best news imaginable.

The great offer of the gospel is adventure. We're God's representatives. We were given a gospel to preach.

The gospel must be shared afresh and told in new ways to every generation. The message of Revelation 14 is to be lived, shared, and proclaimed. We are to tell the world of the everlasting gospel. Christ died to save sinners. We are to warn of a day of judgment: a day of grace for those who trust Christ, and a day of justice for those who do not. And we are to call the world to worship the Creator and Redeemer.

This is our message. This is our hope.

CHAPTER TWELVE

The One Who Avenges You

Revelation 15–18

*A*s we draw closer to earth's final days, ominous times await us. But the clear message of Revelation is, those who trust in Jesus need not fear. In Revelation, chapters 15 through 18, however, we see what happens to those who reject God's final appeal. In these chapters we read of God's wrath upon those who worship the satanic trinity and upon the prostitute Babylon.

As we read these chapters, do not forget the big picture of Revelation: God triumphs over Satan—and His people triumph with Him.

Now let's read of God's wrath against those who reject Him: "I saw in heaven another great and marvelous sign: seven angels with the seven last plagues—last, because with them God's wrath is completed. And I saw what looked like a sea of glass mixed with fire and, standing beside the sea, those who had been victorious over the beast and his image and over the number of his name. They held harps given them by God" (Revelation 15:1, 2).

In verse 2, John sees the redeemed standing in heaven beside the sea of glass. This gives away the end of the story before the story begins. John is using this technique to assure us of the victory and, thus, inspire courage for today's battle.

In verse 1 John warns us that the seven angels are about to pour out the seven last plagues, but before they begin, John pictures the redeemed as though they have already passed through the cataclysmic events that take place before Christ's return. He tells us that those who trust in God are going to get through the plagues without being harmed. Those who are faithful to Jesus will stand triumphant at the end of the day, and worship as they sing "the song of Moses . . . and the song of the Lamb" (Revelation 15:3).

Notice that this song of victory focuses entirely on God.

> "Great and marvelous are your deeds,
>   Lord God Almighty.
> Just and true are your ways,
>   King of the ages.
> Who will not fear you, O Lord,
>   and bring glory to your name?
> For you alone are holy.
> All nations will come
>   and worship before you,
> for your righteous acts have been revealed"
>   (Revelation 15:3, 4).

This song focuses on God and His glory and His worthiness. This is the essence of true worship. True worship always focuses on God. True worship always gives glory to God alone. Those who are faithful to God will worship Him exclusively, and nothing else.

Verse 6 tells us that seven angels who hold the seven last plagues are preparing to pour out God's wrath on the earth. The plagues are reserved for those who have chosen to reject God by disobeying His commandments. The plagues are a response to their refusal to repent.

Verse 8 tells us that no one could enter the temple while the plagues were being poured out. "And the temple was filled with smoke from the glory of God and from his power, and no one could enter the temple until the seven plagues of the seven angels were completed" (Revelation 15:8).

The temple is the place of forgiveness, but that place of forgiveness is closed at this time. Those upon whom the plagues fall have refused God's call to repentance. By this time, the fate of these people has been sealed. The time for mercy has closed.

This is the first time, however, that we see God's wrath unmixed with mercy. God's grace has always diluted His wrath because His judgments have always been designed to bring repentance. That is why God's final punishment of sinners is referred to as "God's strange act." However, there comes a time when God says enough is enough, and probation has closed.

God is merciful, but He will not be merciful forever. A day is coming when those who reject Him will receive their just desserts.

In Revelation 6 the martyrs are pictured as crying out for justice. They ask God how long He will delay the justice that they are due. The seven last plagues are God's answer to their cry.

These plagues are not poured out against God's people. If you are among those who have claimed Jesus as your Lord and Savior and have determined to trust Him and by God's grace to remain faithful to Him, you have nothing to fear from the plagues. The plagues are reserved for those who have rejected God's call to repentance and who have persecuted His people. The plagues are God's undiluted wrath against those who persist in their hatred of God and His people.

> Then I heard a loud voice from the temple saying to the seven angels, "Go, pour out the seven bowls of God's wrath on the earth."
> The first angel went and poured out his bowl on the land, and ugly and painful sores broke out on the people who had the mark of the beast and worshiped his image (Revelation 16:1, 2).

Those who have received the mark of the beast and given their worship to someone other than God will be assailed with painful sores. If you have received the seal of God, these sores will not harm you.

The second angel poured out his bowl on the sea, and it turned into blood like that of a dead man, and every living thing in the sea died.

The third angel poured out his bowl on the rivers and springs of water, and they became blood. Then I heard the angel in charge of the waters say:

> "You are just in these judgments,
>> you who are and who were, the Holy One,
>> because you have so judged;
> for they have shed the blood of your saints and prophets,
>> and you have given them blood to drink as they deserve"
>>>>>>> (Revelation 16:3–6).

These first three plagues are similar to the plagues God poured out on Egypt in order that He might set His people free. Now God uses plagues to set spiritual Israel free from the bondage of sin and of this world, as He takes us to the ultimate Promised Land, heaven. God defeated Egypt with plagues, and now He defeats spiritual Babylon with plagues.

The second and third plagues turn the seas, the rivers, and the springs of water into blood in response to the shedding of the blood of the martyrs that Babylon has shed. Now comes the fourth plague: "The fourth angel poured out his bowl on the sun, and the sun was given power to scorch people with fire. They were seared by the intense heat and they cursed the name of God, who had control over these plagues, but they refused to repent and glorify him" (Revelation 16:8, 9).

No one repents as a result of these plagues. Their hatred of God and His people only intensifies.

It appears obvious that the first four plagues are literal. The next three plagues may actually be taken more spiritually than literally. Whether they are spiritual or literal, their effect is certainly spiritual.

"The fifth angel poured out his bowl on the throne of the beast, and his kingdom was plunged into darkness. Men gnawed their tongues in agony and cursed the God of heaven because of their pains and their sores, but they refused to repent of what they had done" (Revelation 16:10, 11). The fifth plague is different from the first four in that the first four affected the general population while the fifth plague goes directly to "the throne of the beast." This is a supernatural darkness—darkness so intense it causes men to gnaw "their tongues in agony." This is spiritual darkness that results from rejection of the gospel.

"The sixth angel poured out his bowl on the great river Euphrates, and its water was dried up to prepare the way for the kings from the East. Then I saw three evil spirits that looked like frogs; they came out of the mouth of the dragon, out of the mouth of the beast and out of the mouth of the false prophet. They are spirits of demons performing miraculous signs, and they go out to the kings of the whole world, to gather them for the battle on the great day of God Almighty" (Revelation 16:12–14). The sixth plague, the drying up of the river Euphrates, signifies the collapse of end-time Babylon—the religious system that persecutes God's last-day people. History tells us that the ancient Babylonian Empire failed when the Medes and Persians diverted the river and invaded the city through the empty riverbed. Similarly, the collapse of end-time spiritual Babylon is typified by the drying up of the river Euphrates, as biblical commentator Hans LaRondelle suggests. This time the Euphrates must be understood figuratively because it represents the nations that support Babylon. This means that the people and the nations will withdraw their support for Babylon and thus it falls.

The "kings from the East" in verse 12 refer to Christ and His army of the saints. Verse 13 speaks of "three evil spirits that looked like frogs." Frogs symbolize the "unclean."

Verse 14 makes it clear that demonic activity will increase as we near the end. These spirits gather the armies of the world to do battle against Jesus and His army.

The seventh plague is about to be poured out but, first, Jesus has a word of encouragement for His people. "Behold, I come like a thief!

Blessed is he who stays awake and keeps his clothes with him, so that he may not go naked and be shamefully exposed" (Revelation 16:15).

We must remember that the seven last plagues are designed to deliver us and to prepare the world for the return of Jesus, an event of great joy for God's people. The Second Coming will end all of the sickness, sin, and suffering in our world.

One thing will get you through this difficult time, and that is the robe of Christ's righteousness. Do not trust in your own goodness; trust, instead, in the forgiveness of Christ and the salvation He so graciously gives to you. That alone is all you need.

You have nothing to fear from the plagues. Just as ancient Israel was delivered from Egypt by the plagues, you will be too.

In the sixth plague, Christ and His armies, represented by the "kings from the East," go up against satanic forces, represented by the three frogs who gather the kings of the world together for a great battle. The two forces head for a place called Armageddon. "Then they gathered the kings together to the place that in Hebrew is called Armageddon" (Revelation 16:16).

In Palestine, a place known as Megiddo was the site of several decisive battles in the history of ancient Israel. John appears to be borrowing this idea for the last great battle between good and evil at the end of time. This is more of a spiritual than a physical battle. The issues involved in the great struggle between God and Satan are spiritual. It is a clash of ideas, a conflict of loyalties.

The seven last plagues are intended to show us that God and those who trust Him will triumph at the end. Now it is time for the seventh plague: "The seventh angel poured out his bowl into the air, and out of the temple came a loud voice from the throne, saying, 'It is done!' " (Revelation 16:17).

God's throne is located in the temple. God sits on the throne; He alone is sovereign in the universe. God rules over all and will judge all. When the time is right, the voice from the throne of God cries, "It is done!"

When Jesus was crucified, He cried, "It is finished," thus announcing His victory over Satan and sin. Here, the same voice announces, "It is done," to declare the end of earth's history and Christ's ultimate victory over Satan.

> Then there came flashes of lightning, rumblings, peals of thunder and a severe earthquake. No earthquake like it has ever occurred since man has been on earth, so tremendous was the quake. The great city split into three parts, and the cities of the nations collapsed. God remembered Babylon the Great and gave her the cup filled with the wine of the fury of his wrath. Every island fled away and the mountains could not be found. From the sky huge hailstones of about a hundred pounds each fell upon men. And they cursed God on account of the plague of hail, because the plague was so terrible (Revelation 16:18–21).

In verse 19, "the great city" referring to Babylon split into three parts. Then "the cities of the nations collapsed."

Earlier we saw Babylon collapse when the nations withdrew their support. Now we see those nations and religious organizations that supported Babylon collapse as well. Babylon is about to receive the full force of God's wrath.

Hailstones execute God's judgment. If a hailstone weighing a hundred pounds fell from the sky, it would destroy anything it hit. This is a picture of the complete destruction of the satanic trinity, of Babylon, and of the nations that supported her.

The seven last plagues are not given to produce repentance. The time for repentance has passed. This is God's wrath without mercy. God is avenging the innocent blood that has been shed.

But it's not just shed blood that provokes God's wrath. God will avenge Satan's attempts to destroy people through his lies. God hates false doctrine. He hates lies that destroy and rob people of grace.

Satan creates a counterfeit trinity, Babylon, that substitutes a lie for the truth—man-made salvation for God's great gift. This provokes God's wrath as much as does the blood of the martyrs.

God holds truth to be sacred. Solomon said, "Buy the truth and do not sell it; / get wisdom, discipline and understanding" (Proverbs 23:23). And Jesus said, " 'Then you will know the truth, and the truth will set you free' " (John 8:32).

By way of contrast, look at what happens when people believe a lie. Jesus speaks to those who promoted man-made ways of salvation: " 'You belong to your father, the devil, and you want to carry out your father's desire. He was a murderer from the beginning, not holding to the truth, for there is no truth in him. When he lies, he speaks his native language, for he is a liar and the father of lies' " (John 8:44).

And Paul tells us of the results that come when people believe the lie and attempt to win salvation through man-made means. "They exchanged the truth of God for a lie, and worshiped and served created things rather than the Creator—who is forever praised. Amen" (Romans 1:25).

Paul's words foretell of Babylon's attempts to substitute man-made means of salvation for God's one way of salvation. God hates lies, especially those lies that lead people away from salvation, which is why God pours out His wrath on the satanic trinity and on Babylon.

Chapters 17 and 18 give the details of the sixth plague, the drying up of the river Euphrates. This is the plague that results in the fall of Babylon.

Remember that Babylon stands for the apostate religious system allied with the nations and all their political, financial, and military power. Babylon, this union of church and state, persecutes God's last-day people—a people who remain loyal to God and who demonstrate their loyalty by their obedience.

An angel now shows John the destruction of Babylon, but prophecy is not given in order that we might know every detail of the future.

Prophecy is given, instead, so that when what it predicts unfolds, we will remember the prophecy, and as a result, our faith is strengthened. "One of the seven angels who had the seven bowls came and said to me, 'Come, I will show you the punishment of the great prostitute, who sits on many waters. With her the kings of the earth committed adultery and the inhabitants of the earth were intoxicated with the wine of her adulteries' " (Revelation 17:1, 2). Babylon has formed an adulterous alliance with the nations of the earth. Sexual sin and drunkenness symbolize rebellion against God and His truth. John saw Babylon taken to the desert to be destroyed. She bears a rather ominous name.

This title was written on her forehead:

MYSTERY
BABYLON THE GREAT
THE MOTHER OF PROSTITUTES
AND OF THE ABOMINATIONS OF THE EARTH.

I saw that the woman was drunk with the blood of the saints, the blood of those who bore testimony to Jesus (Revelation 17:5, 6).

Babylon is presented as a whore, but the true followers of Christ are represented as "the virgin bride." Eugene Peterson describes the contrast between Satan's counterfeit religious system, the whore of Babylon, and Christ's true church, the virgin bride: "The Bride is as sexual a metaphor as the Whore, but it forms an absolute contrast. For the Whore, sex is in the service of commerce; with the Bride, sex is devoted to love. For the Whore, sex is a contract; for the Bride, sex is a life commitment. For the Whore, sex is a calculation; for the Bride, sex is an offering."

God declared to ancient Israel that He did not desire their sacrifices, that is, the outward trappings of religiosity devoid of genuine love. God said that He desired a sacrifice of the heart. God wants a relationship of love with His people, His chosen bride.

The psalmist declares,

> Sacrifice and offering you did not desire,
>   but my ears you have pierced;
> burnt offerings and sin offerings
>   you did not require. . . .
> "I desire to do your will, O my God;
>   your law is within my heart" (Psalm 40:6, 8).

In verse 6, the psalmist speaks of his ears as having been pierced. When a servant declared his desire to spend the rest of his life in service to his master, his ear was pierced as a sign of the master's ownership. The servant entered into the relationship willingly because of his love for the master. The psalmist understood that what God desires is not an outward relationship of form without heart. God desires a relationship of genuine love—a relationship of the heart.

The rest of chapter 17 contains a detailed description of Babylon, the beast upon which she sits, and kings who rise and fall. Look at what happens next: "They will make war against the Lamb, but the Lamb will overcome them because he is Lord of lords and King of kings—and with him will be his called, chosen and faithful followers" (Revelation 17:14).

Who wins this struggle? The outcome has already been determined. Jesus, the Lamb, will overcome Babylon, the satanic trinity, and the nations who form an alliance with them. Not only does Jesus win, but His faithful followers are victorious right along with the Lamb.

Jesus is declared to be "Lord of lords and King of kings." The Lamb of God is victorious, and He will reign forever and ever!

God longs for everyone to join Him in the triumphant march of the Lamb to victory. He longs that we be spared the fate of the satanic trinity and Babylon, so He issues an impassioned plea to those whose lives still stand in the balance.

Then I heard another voice from heaven say:

"Come out of her, my people,
    so that you will not share in her sins,
    so that you will not receive any of her plagues"
                           (Revelation 18:4).

It is not God's desire that any suffer the fate of Babylon but that all come to salvation, and so He pleads that we reject the lie and accept the truth. The truth is simply this: Jesus Christ loves you, died to save you, is returning for you, and will see you through all manner of evil if you will but trust Him. And you will join that multitude who worship the Lamb by singing

"Hallelujah!
Salvation and glory and power belong to our God,
    for true and just are his judgments.
He has condemned the great prostitute
    who corrupted the earth by her adulteries.
He has avenged on her the blood of his servants." . . .
"Hallelujah!
    For our Lord God Almighty reigns"
                          (Revelation 19:1, 2, 6).

This is a song of complete victory. Only those who have accepted Christ as their Lord and Savior will sing it. Only those who know the joy of God's great gift of grace will sing. But no one who has received the gift will be able to remain silent. They will all sing and praise the One who made their salvation complete.

I choose to be among them. How about you?

Chapter Thirteen

The One Who Is Your Bridegroom

Revelation 19–21

anko Stefanovic tells us that during a wedding in Palestine in Bible times, the groom would go to the bride's house to pay the dowry. The couple was considered to be married after the father of the bride had received the dowry. The wedding ceremony may not have taken place yet, and the couple was not yet sharing the same house or bed, but they were, for all intents and purposes, married.

After paying the dowry, the groom would return to his father's house to prepare the house for the wedding. The bride remained in her father's house and prepared herself. Once both bride and groom had completed their preparations, the wedding ceremony could begin.

Recently, I was able to observe a modern example of this up close when my daughter was married. Although our event took place nearly two millennia after John wrote Revelation, the similarities were many even though culture and customs are quite different. My wife and both of my daughters spent untold hours preparing the house, the church, and the reception hall for the wedding. Then my daughter, along with a team of friends, prepared herself for her groom. Everything else in our lives was placed on hold until the wedding had taken place.

This is what John had in mind when he spoke of the wedding of the Lamb. The entire book of Revelation points forward to one consummating event, the wedding feast of the Lamb. Those who think that Armageddon is the consummating event of Revelation have missed the point. Everything points forward to the wedding feast of the Lamb.

> Then I heard what sounded like a great multitude, like the roar of rushing waters and like loud peals of thunder, shouting:
>
> "Hallelujah!
> For our Lord God Almighty reigns.
> Let us rejoice and be glad
> and give him glory!
> For the wedding of the Lamb has come,
> and his bride has made herself ready.
> Fine linen, bright and clean,
> was given her to wear."
> (Fine linen stands for the righteous acts of the saints.)
> (Revelation 19:6–8).

Jesus paid the dowry with His life on Calvary. At that point, the church was married to Jesus, the Bridegroom.

Jesus told His disciples that He would "go to prepare a place." He ascended to heaven to make preparations for the wedding ceremony.

Those who have committed themselves to Jesus constitute the bride. When you accepted Christ's sacrifice for your sins, you accepted the dowry. You were then married to Christ.

Now, as Jesus prepares a place in His Father's house for the wedding, you are to prepare yourself for this great event. You prepare by adorning yourself with white linen. The white linen is the righteousness of Christ.

Soon the Bridegroom will return in order to take you to His Father's house so you can celebrate your marriage. The Groom returns at what Scripture calls the second coming of Jesus. John describes that event:

> I saw heaven standing open and there before me was a white horse, whose rider is called Faithful and True. With justice he judges and makes war. His eyes are like blazing fire, and on his head are many crowns. He has a name written on him that no one knows but he himself. He is dressed in a robe dipped in blood, and his name is the Word of God (Revelation 19:11–13).

The One who is "called Faithful and True" is Jesus. He wears many crowns because He is ruler over all and has conquered all. Jesus is returning to claim His chosen bride so that they can celebrate their marriage. This wedding is the culminating act of everything Christ has sacrificed and done. This has been His sole objective—to enjoy intimacy with you forever!

In contrast to the marriage feast of the Lamb is the "great supper of God." Scripture tells us that when Jesus comes there will be two groups of people alive on earth: those eagerly awaiting His coming and those who do not want Him to return. Those who long to see Him will be wearing the fine linen, the righteousness of Jesus.

Those who have rejected Jesus, and have rebelled against Him, have reason to fear because Scripture tells us that they will be killed by the brightness of the Second Coming (see 2 Thessalonians 2:8). But for those—both living and dead—who have accepted Jesus as their Savior and have given themselves to Him, Jesus' return is a glorious event. Here is what the apostle Paul tells us will take place for them at that time: "For the Lord himself will come down from heaven, with a loud command, with the voice of the archangel and with the trumpet call of God, and the dead in Christ will rise first. After that, we who are still alive and are left will be caught up together with them in the clouds to meet the Lord in the air. And so we will be with the Lord forever" (1 Thessalonians 4:16, 17).

But what happens to the other group—those who are killed by the brightness of Jesus' coming? John describes a gruesome scene as the birds feed on their dead bodies: "And I saw an angel standing in the sun, who cried in a loud voice to all the birds flying in midair, 'Come, gather together for the great supper of God, so that you may eat the flesh of kings, generals, and mighty men, of horses and their riders, and the flesh of all people, free and slave, small and great' " (Revelation 19:17, 18).

When we compare 1 Thessalonians with Revelation 19 and other passages of the Bible, we find that when Jesus comes the second time there will actually be four groups of people on earth: First, there are those who are alive on the earth when Jesus comes, and in this group, some will be saved and ready to meet Jesus, while others will not be ready to meet Him and will be lost. Also, there are those who have died before Jesus comes. And again, some of these will be saved, and some will be lost. So we have four distinct groups—the living who are saved and the living who are lost; the dead who are saved and the dead who are lost.

When Jesus returns, the living who are saved will ascend to meet Him in the air. The living who are lost will be killed by the brightness of His coming. The dead who are saved will be resurrected in what the Scripture calls the "first resurrection" to live with Jesus forever. The dead who are lost will not be disturbed by the Second Coming; they will sleep on, waiting for what the Bible describes as a "second death," which will follow the final day of judgment: "(The rest of the dead did not come to life until the thousand years were ended.) This is the first resurrection. Blessed and holy are those who have part in the first resurrection. The second death has no power over them, but they will be priests of God and of Christ and will reign with him for a thousand years" (Revelation 20:5, 6).

But what happens to Satan and his demons when Jesus returns? "And I saw an angel coming down out of heaven, having the key to the Abyss and holding in his hand a great chain. He seized the dragon, that ancient serpent, who is the devil, or Satan, and bound him for a thousand years. He threw him into the Abyss, and locked and sealed it over him, to keep him from deceiving the nations anymore until the thousand years were ended. After that, he must be set free for a short time" (Revelation 20:1–3). The abyss is the place where Satan and his demons are confined against their will. At the second coming of Jesus, Satan and the fallen angels are not destroyed but are confined to the abyss.

Satan and the fallen angels are chained, not with literal chains, but by a chain of circumstance, and are confined to this planet, which becomes, for them, the abyss. The circumstances which bind Satan and the fallen angels are the facts that everyone who has rejected God is dead, and those who have accepted Him are taken to heaven with Jesus.

This leaves no one for Satan to tempt. He and his angels have nothing to do but to think about the damage their rebellion has caused. John tells us that they will be confined to this planet for a thousand years. This is called the millennium, which begins after the Second Coming and ends prior to the final judgment and the destruction of Satan and his fallen angels.

John tells us that those who have sided with God against the counterfeit trinity will be given authority to judge. This is at least a part of what we will do while in heaven for the millennium. At the end of the thousand years, Satan will be released from his prison. How does that happen? "(The rest of the dead did not come to life until the thousand years were ended.) This is the first resurrection" (Revelation 20:5).

Those who have rejected Jesus in favor of the counterfeit trinity are raised to life at the end of the millennium. Satan now has someone to tempt, and he goes back to work with a vengeance. Those who have been faithful to God and have spent the millennium with Him in heaven will return with Christ to earth after the thousand years have passed. We will be in the Holy City, the New Jerusalem. Satan will gather together everyone who, throughout the history of the earth, has rejected God. He will attempt to take the New Jerusalem by force.

What happens? "They marched across the breadth of the earth and surrounded the camp of God's people, the city he loves. But fire came down from heaven and devoured them" (Revelation 20:9).

A final judgment will then take place. "And I saw the dead, great and small, standing before the throne, and books were opened. Another book was opened, which is the book of life. The dead were judged according to what they had done as recorded in the books" (Revelation 20:12).

At the end of the judgment, sin and sinner will be completely eliminated. "If anyone's name was not found written in the book of life, he was thrown into the lake of fire" (Revelation 20:15).

Notice that those whose names are written in the book of life are not destroyed. Perish the thought! They comprise the chosen bride of the Lamb! Why would the Groom destroy His bride, His cherished one?

If the book of Revelation is all about revealing Jesus Christ, this may be the most important picture John could give. It is the picture of Jesus longing for you. Jesus' ultimate objective in the universe is to establish uninterrupted fellowship with you. You are a part of Jesus' chosen bride. The Groom would never harm the bride. He longs to cherish and protect the bride. He longs to spend eternity with her.

As of this writing, Gayle and I have been married for nearly thirty-one years. My memories of our wedding day are vivid.

I was standing in the front of the church in Tulsa, Oklahoma, in a rented tuxedo. Even though it was the twenty-eighth of December and rather cold and rainy, I was sweating profusely. I stood for what seemed to be an eternity watching an endless stream of bridesmaids march down the isle.

Then the doors at the back of the church closed. I got real nervous about then. I could scarcely breathe. My knees trembled, my palms were sweaty, my heart raced, and my mouth was dry.

Finally, those doors opened again, revealing the most beautiful sight I have ever seen. Gayle was positively radiant! The dress was beautiful, her hair was beautiful, and she was beautiful.

Then Gayle took that long, slow walk down the isle. I thought that walk would never end! I wanted my bride. I longed to take her arm, hold her hand, repeat our vows, and begin our lives together.

Eventually, Gayle arrived. Her smile put the glimmer of diamonds to shame. She took my arm, and my heart really began to pound.

Think of the array of emotions I experienced that day. I felt love, anticipation, anxiety, impatience, longing, desire, and hope. I wanted to be with Gayle. I wanted to live with her.

When Jesus decided to tell us about heaven, the New Jerusalem, and the earth made new, He used the language of intimate relationship. He used the language of a wedding.

Jesus is the Groom; the church is His bride. Jesus feels all the emotions toward His bride that I felt toward Gayle that day, only multiplied by billions. Once you are able to get your mind around that, then you begin to get a small idea of what Jesus feels toward us.

We who believe in the Lamb comprise His chosen bride. No one has been forced to come to the marriage. The grace of the Lamb is triumphant, but that grace has not compelled men and women to believe. His grace woos us but does not force us. Jesus does not bring us as slaves to the king, the spoils of war, but as the bride who will dwell with her husband. Jesus wants to live with the bride!

Jesus uses the language of intimate relationship when describing heaven. He wasn't thinking of the beauty of the city and He wasn't thinking of the precious materials used in the construction of the city. The first and most important thing on His mind was His bride, the church.

When God thinks of heaven, He thinks about you!

What do you think about when you think about heaven? Heaven is the presence of Jesus.

Keep the streets of gold, the walls of jasper, and the gates of pearl. You can keep my mansion, my harp, and my crown. Just let me live in the presence of Jesus, and that is heaven enough for me!

Augustine of Hippo said, "Heaven is the perfectly ordered and harmonious enjoyment of God and of one another in God."

It will be heaven just to be in the presence of the One who loves us and died to save us. The imagery of relationship continues in verse 3: "And I heard a loud voice from the throne saying, 'Now the dwelling of God is with men, and he will live with them. They will be his people, and God himself will be with them and be their God. He will wipe every tear from their eyes. There will be no more death or mourning or crying or pain, for the old order of things has passed away' " (Revelation 21:3, 4).

After the wedding was over, I didn't say to Gayle, "Well, that was nice. I guess I'll go home now. I'll call you in a couple of days. Bye!" That would have been unthinkable!

Gayle and I moved in together. We began to live together, to experience each other every day.

That is what Jesus wants for His bride. Jesus wants to live with you.

Revelation 21:3 is a restatement of a promise found in the Old Testament book of Ezekiel. "My dwelling place will be with them; I will be their God, and they will be my people" (Ezekiel 37:27). God made the same promise through Jeremiah: "They will be my people, and I will be their God. . . . I will make an everlasting covenant with them: I will never stop doing good to them, and I will inspire them to fear me, so that they will never turn away from me" (Jeremiah 32:38, 40).

Look at these other promises God has given us:

> And the ransomed of the LORD will return.
> They will enter Zion with singing;
>   everlasting joy will crown their heads.
> Gladness and joy will overtake them,
>   and sorrow and sighing will flee away (Isaiah 35:10).

> "I will rejoice over Jerusalem
>   and take delight in my people;
> the sound of weeping and of crying
>   will be heard in it no more" (Isaiah 65:19).

> He will swallow up death forever.
> The Sovereign LORD will wipe away the tears
>   from all faces;
> he will remove the disgrace of his people
>   from all the earth.
> The LORD has spoken (Isaiah 25:8).

These promises reflect what has been Jesus' desire for you for millennia. He longs to live with you and make you happy. Wherever you are is the place He will call home.

My wife's family has lived in the same house for nearly fifty years. They've lived there long enough that none of the children can ever remember the Whitacres living anywhere else. They sometimes refer to it as "our house," but more often they refer to it as "home." What makes it home isn't the address or the lot or the garage or the architecture. What makes it home is the people.

You may live in a bigger or newer or better house than the Whitacres do, but as nice as your house may be, they would never refer to your house as home because the people who are most important to them don't live there.

It is the people in the relationships that makes home "home." The streets of gold, great fountains, lots of fun, and no smog, are not the things that make heaven "heaven." All of that is perfectly true, but they are not the things that make it heaven.

Actually, I think that heaven is far greater than our wildest imagination. The same God who designed the best of everything in this world also designed heaven, only He took it to a far greater extent than anything we've ever seen. Yet, that's still not what makes heaven "heaven."

What makes heaven "heaven" is Jesus. Heaven is being there with Him. With His presence comes peace and contentment, a fulfillment, a sense that all is well. That is also a contentment that bubbles over into the rest of life.

We can anticipate this future in the presence of Jesus; we can be with Him in a place where everything He wants happens the way He wants. Jesus wants to live with you. And when He does, it will feel like home.

When many savings and loan institutions failed in 1989, the federal government had to dispose of numerous properties. The most interesting one was the six-acre McCune mansion in Paradise Valley, Arizona. Walker McCune built the house in the 1960s for his young bride. The house contains fifty-three thousand square feet and includes an ice skating rink, an Olympic swimming pool, a fourteen-car garage, its own beauty salon, guest house, and a ballroom with an eighty-thousand-dollar chandelier.

Oddly enough, Mrs. McCune didn't like it and never moved in.

Perhaps there are others who don't like Paradise Valley, Arizona, but no one will be dissatisfied with the mansion Christ has prepared for His bride. We will be satisfied because we will be living with God, and God will be living with us. When we live with God, we will feel at home.

Revelation 21:7 tells us how to make certain that our home is in heaven: "He who overcomes will inherit all this, and I will be his God and he will be my son."

How do we get to heaven? We must be "overcomers." Revelation 12:11 says, "They overcame him / by the blood of the Lamb."

Overcoming always has to do with what Jesus has done, and what Jesus can do through us. I'm not going to heaven because I've preached to crowds of people around the world, or because I've preached on television. I'm going to heaven because Christ died on that cross.

None of us are going to heaven because we're good. We're not going to heaven because we've worked hard to get there. We're not going to heaven because we pray and accept Christ. We're going to heaven because of what Jesus did on the cross.

If we will trust in the blood of the Lamb—if we will repent and humbly obey—we will inherit all things. Better yet, God says, "I will be his God and he will be my son."

Again, Jesus uses the language of intimacy and relationship. He calls us His bride, and now He calls us His son. It is significant that the word *son* is used. When the book of Revelation was written, daughters could not inherit their father's wealth. Only a son could inherit that which belonged to his father.

Jesus tells us that "overcomers"—men and women alike—will be His sons, and therefore will inherit all that our Father has to offer. No one who repents and obeys will be left out. God calls you His son, and He wants to give you everything He owns.

Paul tells us that when we are assured of Christ as our Savior and Lord, we are enabled to say, "*Abba*"—"Father." *Abba* is a Hebrew word that is more intimate than our word *daddy*. A small child refers to his father in the most intimate of terms, "daddy." If we trust in the blood of the Lamb, we can call God "Daddy"—"*Abba*," or "Father."

We are surprised once again by the intimate language used to describe our relationship to God! This is the language of relationships. It is the language of intimate fellowship.

God wants to live with you. When that happens, when we find ourselves living with God, it will feel like home. You were made to live with God. You were made for heaven.

Today you are one day nearer to home than ever before. One day nearer the dawning when the fog will lift, mysteries clear, and all question marks straighten up into exclamation points!

You will see the King! You will live with God, and feel at home!

What do you think of heaven? What do you think it will be like to live there?

Looking forward to the eternal world is not a form of escapism or wishful thinking. It is what a Christian is meant to do.

We get to heaven by recognizing that we don't deserve it but that Jesus does. And, as we trust in the blood of the Lamb, and receive Jesus as our Lord and Savior, we too will live with God. We become His bride. We become sons of God. Though we live on earth, we have already established legal residence in heaven.

In the last century, an American tourist paid a visit to a renowned Polish rabbi, Hofetz Chaim. He was astonished to see that the rabbi's home was only a simple room filled with books, plus a table and a cot.

The tourist asked, "Rabbi, where is your furniture?"

Hofetz Chaim replied, "Where is yours?"

The puzzled American asked, "Mine? But I'm only a visitor here. I'm only passing through."

The rabbi replied, "So am I."

Where is your home? Do you plan to be in heaven? Are you a part of the bride of God? Are you a son of God?

The Groom wants to live with you. He cherishes you and longs for an eternity of intimacy with you. He is coming again to take you to His home so you can live with Him there. And when He does, you'll feel right at home.

CHAPTER FOURTEEN

The One Who Prepares a Home for You

Revelation 22

*T*hus far, John has outlined earth's final hours. He has shown us how things will end. But, most importantly, he has shown us Jesus.

Jesus is the Bridegroom who longs for His bride, which is you. When Jesus ascended to heaven, He did so to "prepare a place for you." He also said that He would come again to get us so that we could be with Him forever. That is what He told His disciples. Now John attempts to describe the place the Bridegroom has prepared for His bride.

As we study these chapters in the book of Revelation, it is important that we keep the wedding customs of the East in mind. Remember, the groom goes to the home of the father of the bride in order to pay the dowry. Once the dowry is paid, the couple is thought of as married, but the groom returns to his father's house to prepare for the wedding itself.

The bride, meanwhile, remains at her home in order to prepare for the wedding. She bathes, anoints herself with perfumes, and puts on white linen clothes.

When all is ready, the wedding feast is celebrated in the home of the father of the groom:

> Then I saw a new heaven and a new earth, for the first
> heaven and the first earth had passed away, and there was no

longer any sea. I saw the Holy City, the new Jerusalem, coming down out of heaven from God, prepared as a bride beautifully dressed for her husband. And I heard a loud voice from the throne saying, "Now the dwelling of God is with men, and he will live with them. They will be his people, and God himself will be with them and be their God. He will wipe every tear from their eyes. There will be no more death or mourning or crying or pain, for the old order of things has passed away" (Revelation 21:1–4).

These final chapters describe the place the Bridegroom has prepared for His bride. Jesus is preparing His Father's house for the wedding feast. He is making preparations for His marriage to you, His church, His bride.

Have you ever wondered why there will be no more sea in the new earth that God is preparing for us? John was writing of a day of reunion between God and His children. But it will also be a day of reunion between us and our loved ones and friends. People you love who have been separated from you by death or distance will then be reunited with you—forever.

John began to think of all the people he had been separated from. John wrote this book while imprisoned on the island of Patmos. The sea formed his prison walls; it was the sea that separated John from the people he loved. So can you just imagine how John must have felt when the Lord showed him that there would be no more sea in the new world that He would create for His people? To John—and to us—it speaks of no more separation. Never again will you be separated from those you love—and never again will you be separated from Jesus.

Just to make certain that John understood and that we will have confidence that this day will indeed come, Jesus said, " 'It is done. I am the Alpha and the Omega, the Beginning and the End. To him who is thirsty I will give to drink without cost from the spring of the water of life. He who overcomes will inherit all this, and I will be his God and he will be my son' " (Revelation 21:6, 7).

Jesus tells us that He is everything to us. He is the beginning, the end, the first, the last, and everything in between. That means that He is fully capable of accomplishing what He has promised. He says that you are the rightful heir of heaven. If we hold fast to Jesus, we will inherit heaven.

Jesus also uses every human relationship of intimacy possible: He has called us His friends, His brothers, His bride, His heirs, and now He calls us sons. He has done everything possible to show us how close He feels to us and how intimate our relationship with Him can be.

Then one of the angels who had held one of the bowls with the last plagues took John to the top of a mountain to show him the New Jerusalem, the city of God. Here is how John described what he saw.

> It shone with the glory of God, and its brilliance was like that of a very precious jewel, like a jasper, clear as crystal. It had a great, high wall with twelve gates, and with twelve angels at the gates. On the gates were written the names of the twelve tribes of Israel. There were three gates on the east, three on the north, three on the south and three on the west. The wall of the city had twelve foundations, and on them were the names of the twelve apostles of the Lamb. . . .
>
> . . . The wall was made of jasper, and the city of pure gold, as pure as glass. The foundations of the city walls were decorated with every kind of precious stone. . . . The twelve gates were twelve pearls, each gate made of a single pearl. The great street of the city was of pure gold, like transparent glass. . . .
>
> . . . The city does not need the sun or the moon to shine on it, for the glory of God gives it light, and the Lamb is its lamp (Revelation 21:11–14, 18, 19, 21, 23).

Words cannot adequately describe the glories of that city. Have you ever wondered why Jesus has prepared a place so extravagant? After all do we really need gates of pearl, foundations of precious stones, walls of jasper, and streets of gold? Aren't these things unnecessary?

Not when you are talking about lovers.

Do you remember the first time you knew you were in love—*really* knew you were in love? How much was too much to give to your lover? Was anything too good for the one you loved?

Did you ever make yourself look just a little foolish with your exuberance for the object of your affection? Or what about the first time you looked into the face of your newborn baby? How much was too much to do for that child?

That's what this description of heaven and the New Jerusalem is all about. Jesus is so much in love with you that nothing is too good for you! He gives and gives and gives.

One of the Hebrew words in the Old Testament for "love" is *hessed*, which refers to a love stronger and more passionate than any earthly love, a love that knows no bounds. That's why, when Jesus the Bridegroom went to heaven to prepare a place for you, His chosen bride, He prepared a place that is so opulent as to make you blush. He spared no expense and stopped at nothing.

Why else would He use pure, transparent gold as paving stones? Why else would He prepare a mansion for you in a city that is nothing more than a collection of mansions surrounding the throne of God? Why else would Jesus make the walls of jasper and cause the entire city to shine like gold so pure it looks like transparent glass?

But the description is not finished yet. Feel the emotion; experience the thrill as Jesus sends us a word-picture of what His love has caused Him to prepare for His bride:

> Then the angel showed me the river of the water of life, as clear as crystal, flowing from the throne of God and of the Lamb down the middle of the great street of the city. On each

side of the river stood the tree of life, bearing twelve crops of fruit, yielding its fruit every month. And the leaves of the tree are for the healing of the nations. No longer will there be any curse. The throne of God and of the Lamb will be in the city, and his servants will serve him. They will see his face, and his name will be on their foreheads. There will be no more night. They will not need the light of a lamp or the light of the sun, for the Lord God will give them light. And they will reign for ever and ever (Revelation 22:1–5).

These passages reveal to us the heart of Jesus. We know His desire, His longing, and His preoccupation. It is all for you, for you are a part of that group of people He calls His bride. Listen to the excitement in His voice. " 'Behold, I am coming soon! Blessed is he who keeps the words of the prophecy in this book' " (Revelation 22:7). He's so excited He repeats Himself. " 'Behold, I am coming soon! My reward is with me, and I will give to everyone according to what he has done' " (Revelation 22:12). And yet again the excitement shows through His words: "He who testifies to these things says, 'Yes, I am coming soon' " (Revelation 22:20).

It's as though Jesus is the Fiancé who can hardly wait to see His betrothed, so He writes her every day, saying the same thing each time: "I'm coming soon! It won't be long now and we can be together. I'm coming soon!"

But there are those who do not share the Bridegroom's love. Although the dowry has been paid and they legally belong to the Bridegroom, there are those who have played the harlot and chased after other lovers.

The Bridegroom will never force anyone to accept His entreaties of love. He takes only those who freely choose to love Him back. He will not force. But He will not allow anyone to leave without one last plea. One last time, before John ends his book, he shares the Bridegroom's fervent appeal: John shares the last lines of the Bridegroom's love letter. Listen to the pleading, and the passion, of the Bridegroom. "The

Spirit and the bride say, 'Come!' And let him who hears say, 'Come!' Whoever is thirsty, let him come; and whoever wishes, let him take the free gift of the water of life" (Revelation 22:17).

If you haven't yet accepted the invitation of the Bridegroom, why not make today the day you accept His proposal? Why not make this the day you surrender your heart to His great love? Why not accept of the free gift of the water of life?

When you do, and when you experience His love, you will share His anticipation of the approaching celebration. You will find yourself scarcely able to wait for the wedding feast of the Lamb. And you, like John, will cry, "Amen. Come, Lord Jesus" (Revelation 22:20).

Chapter Fifteen

The One Who Comes for You

Revelation 22

*I*n 1241, the Tatars invaded Poland's old city of Kraków. It was the custom in that city for the hours to be marked, not by a bell, but by a trumpeter. On the hour, every hour, a trumpeter would play a brief song. But on that day in 1241, an arrow cut short the trumpeter's song right in the middle. To this day, you can still hear the trumpeter, his song never finished, ending abruptly. At noon each day, the same haunting call is broadcast on Polish radio—and the trumpet call is never finished.

There is another trumpet song that will be sounded one day. That song is to be played by the angel Gabriel. When Gabriel plays his song, the world will end. No one will stop him. When Gabriel begins his song, he will finish it. Nothing is going to cut it short.

Holocaust survivor Corrie ten Boom said, "We are not a post-war generation, but a pre-peace generation. Jesus is coming."

I wish I could take you today to a graphic portrayal of the Word of God in a great cathedral in Milan. There we would come in out of the glare of the Italian sunshine, pass through the cathedral doors, and suddenly see stretching out before us Europe's third largest cathedral. Here fifty-two marbled columns hold up the lofty, octagonal dome, with over 4,400 turrets and pinnacles. Statues of angels rise all about us, and the effect is one of an incomparable combination of grace and grandeur, beauty and vastness.

Up front, behind the altar, like a window opening out of heaven, is one of the largest stained-glass windows in the world. Depicted here is not an Old Testament scene. That stained-glass window does not depict the resurrection of Jesus Christ the Lord, not His crucifixion nor His ascension. With tremendous imagery, the window depicts the final triumph of Jesus as depicted in the book of Revelation.

The afternoon sun strains in, turning the window into a sea of glass mingled with fire. As you look, you see the vials being outpoured, the trumpets, and Michael and His angels in battle against the dragon. Also there is the great angel with the rainbow upon his head and one foot upon the earth and the other upon the heavens, declaring in the name of Him who lives forever and ever that time shall be no longer. Bound with a chain, Satan is thrown into the bottomless pit at last.

The great white throne glows in the sunlight. Most impressive of all is the great, white horse. Upon the horse sits a still greater Rider with the armies of heaven behind Him. He comes to set everything straight—at last—for all who have hoped in Him, for all who have been subjected to the pain and prejudice of living for Jesus Christ.

The scene depicted in the stained-glass window in that great cathedral is the ultimate triumph of Jesus as Lord and King! It is a scene from the book of Revelation of the return of Jesus to this earth in power and glory!

The book of Revelation closes with one final reference to that great day. The entire New Testament has taken us on a great journey. The immense step from the Babe at Bethlehem to the living, reigning triumphant Lord Jesus, returning to earth for His own people—that is the glorious truth proclaimed throughout Scripture. As the bells ring out the joys of Christmas, may we also be alert for the final trumpet that will announce His return, when we shall always be with Him.

This is how the book of Revelation ends. As we look at the ending of this book, allow me to ask you three questions regarding the Second Coming: When will Jesus return? Why is He coming back? And how can you be ready?

Let's deal with the first question:

> The angel said to me, "These words are trustworthy and true. The Lord, the God of the spirits of the prophets, sent his angel to show his servants the things that must soon take place."
>
> "Behold, I am coming soon! Blessed is he who keeps the words of the prophecy in this book" (Revelation 22:6, 7).

Jesus speaks four times in the final chapter of Revelation, and on three of those four occasions—in verses 7, 12, and 20—He tells us that He is returning quickly.

Jesus has promised to return soon, but what does that mean? How soon is soon?

Look at this quotation from a prominent church leader regarding the return of Jesus. "I hope that the day is near at hand when the advent of the great God will appear, for all things everywhere are boiling, burning, moving, falling, sinking, groaning."

Who do you think wrote that? Was it Chuck Swindoll? Maybe eminent theologian John Stott? Perhaps it was Christian writer Max Lucado?

No, it was Martin Luther, who lived from 1483 to 1546. Over 450 years ago, Martin Luther thought that the time was right for Jesus to return. He expected it! He hoped for it. And that was over 450 years ago!

The church to which I belong was officially formed in 1863. Our church was formed for the purpose of proclaiming the second advent of our Lord Jesus Christ. But we have been preaching of the imminent return for over 140 years. Obviously, God's calculation of "soon" and my calculation of "soon" are very different.

John wrote the book of Revelation 1,900 years ago, yet Jesus said that He was coming "quickly." What that means is that we cannot predict when Jesus will come.

There is renewed interest today in the end of the world and the second coming of Jesus. A few years ago, with the advent of the year

2000 and the Y2K problem, people were talking about the end of the world. I remember hearing a radio program about the book of Revelation and the end of the world.

The current attitude of most people toward the end of the world can be expressed by two bumper stickers I saw while waiting at a red light. The car ahead of me had two stickers, one on the left side of the bumper and one on the right. The one on the left read, "JESUS IS COMING!" and the one on the right read, "ESCAPE TO WISCONSIN." However accidental, this combined message does express what many are thinking about the end of the world.

When is Jesus coming again? I hope very soon. This afternoon is not too soon for me. The fact is, however, no one knows, and anyone who tells you that he or she does is someone to be avoided at all costs.

The second question is, "Why is Jesus coming?" Look at what Jesus Himself says: " 'Behold, I am coming soon! My reward is with me, and I will give to everyone according to what he has done' " (Revelation 22:12). Jesus comes to give a reward. Those who are right with God will get one reward, and all others another. But the main purpose is to reward those who love and serve Him. Jesus said, " 'In my Father's house are many rooms; if it were not so, I would have told you. I am going there to prepare a place for you. And if I go and prepare a place for you, I will come back and take you to be with me that you also may be where I am' " (John 14:2, 3).

Jesus wants to give you a mansion—one you can live in for eternity. But most of all, Jesus wants to be with you. " 'I will come back,' " He said, " 'and take you to be with me that you also may be where I am.' " Jesus wants to receive you to Himself. He wants to be where you are. He never wants to be separated from you again.

Heaven is the presence of Jesus. The church of the first century understood this. They longed to enjoy uninterrupted fellowship with Jesus. They thought more about the second coming of Jesus Christ than about death or about heaven.

Why is Jesus coming again? Jesus longs to be with you, that's why.

The last question is, "What must I do to be ready for the return?" "I, John, am the one who heard and saw these things. And when I had heard and seen them, I fell down to worship at the feet of the angel who had been showing them to me. But he said to me, 'Do not do it! I am a fellow servant with you and with your brothers the prophets and of all who keep the words of this book. Worship God!' " (Revelation 22:8, 9).

The only way to heaven is through faith in the blood of Jesus, which leads to the heartfelt worship of God. The worship of God implies an acknowledgment that God must be Lord of our lives. If Jesus is not Lord of my life, He is not Lord at all. We must acknowledge that He is supreme, the Creator, Sustainer, Redeemer, and Sanctifier of those who trust in Him. We must confess our need of Him because of our sinfulness, and then receive pardon and grace. We must trust in the blood of the Lamb if we are to be ready for the return of Jesus. We get to heaven by the grace of God, and nothing else. This is so important that the last idea in the book of Revelation—the closing concept in the Bible—is the concept of *grace.* "The grace of the Lord Jesus be with God's people. Amen" (Revelation 22:21).

The Bible ends with the concept of grace, God's unmerited favor toward you. Why? Because grace is God's appointed vehicle for your salvation; in fact, it's the only means of our salvation. Paul wrote, "For it is by grace you have been saved, through faith—and this not from yourselves, it is the gift of God—not by works, so that no one can boast" (Ephesians 2:8, 9).

Do you want to get to heaven? Trust in the grace of God! This is the clear message of the Bible.

No matter what else you might have been taught, the Bible says we must trust in the blood of the Lamb as the only way to salvation. Our works can never do it for us because our works can never be good enough to pay the cost. Christ's substitutionary death paid it—in full!

Because of the merits of Christ's death, you can be the recipient of grace.

Christ is perfect—not you; Christ paid the cost—not you. That is grace!

God's grace grants you freedom from sin and freedom from the second death, the death that separates us from God for eternity.

In the late summer of 1989 one million people in Latvia, Lithuania, and Estonia linked arms and formed a human chain 360 miles long. When the chain was completed, one word was passed along the line. Each one spoke to the next until that one word had been passed along all those 360 miles. The word was "freedom"!

When our Lord Jesus Christ cried from the cross, "It is finished!" He might as well have said "Freedom!" Freedom from sin, freedom from ourselves, freedom from death and the grave were all won on the cross and celebrated in the Resurrection.

We opened this chapter with three questions about the second coming of Jesus—when is He coming, why is He coming, and what do we have to do in order to get ready for His coming? The short answers are these:

- When is He coming? Only God knows.
- Why is He coming? To get you so that you can live in His presence forever.
- And what should we do to get ready? Trust in God's grace.

I read of a poor peasant in the mountains who, month after month, year after year, through a long period of declining life, opened his door every morning as soon as he awoke, looking toward the east to see if Jesus Christ were coming. He did not know the date of Christ's coming or he would not have needed to look at all. He was ready for Christ's coming or he would not have been in such a hurry to seek Him. He was hopeful for Christ's coming or he would rather have looked another way. He loved Christ or Christ would not have been His first thought of the morning.

His Master did not come, and eventually the man fell into the sleep of death. But he did so with no panic and no fear.

The same preparation he had made for the coming of Christ each day sufficed as his preparation for death. Often, we awaken in the morning, weary and encumbered with troubled thoughts, and our Father's secret presence comes to mind. We look up to feel the glories of that last morning, when the trumpet shall sound and the dead shall arise indestructible. There will be no weary limbs to bear the spirit down, no feverish dreams to haunt the vision, no dark forecasting of the day's events, and no returning memory of yesterday's sorrows.

God doesn't want anyone to be left out. That's why the final chapter of Revelation has an invitation for you to come to Jesus and look forward to the Second Coming with eager anticipation.

"The Spirit and the bride say, 'Come!' And let him who hears say, 'Come!' Whoever is thirsty, let him come; and whoever wishes, let him take the free gift of the water of life" (Revelation 22:17). This invitation is for you. The Holy Spirit—through the bride, the church—invites you to come to Jesus, to come to heaven.

Everyone who hears the words of this book must also issue the invitation to come as well. If you are thirsty for that which this world cannot quench; if you have a desire—a longing deep in your heart—for something better, then you are invited to take the water of life as a gift from the hand of God.

I have drunk of the water of life freely. I am a recipient of God's grace. The moment I realized that God existed, I knew I could not do otherwise than to live for Him alone. As a recipient of grace myself, I invite you today to partake of it as well.

CHAPTER SIXTEEN

The One Who Helps You Sleep at Night

*A*t the beginning of this book I told you that when I was a boy, Revelation frightened me. I was a Revelation fear-aholic. It gave me nightmares.

As you can now see, I feel differently. Indeed, I can use Revelation as a bedtime story book. Revelation puts my mind at ease and helps me rest in Jesus.

This doesn't mean that horrible things have not happened to God's people down through the ages. It doesn't mean that horrible things aren't happening to God's people today. And it doesn't mean that horrible things won't happen to God's people before the Second Coming. But it does mean that, through it all, I can be confident that Jesus will hold me in His strong hand. I can rest secure in the knowledge that nothing can separate me from the love and acceptance of Christ, my Savior.

Maybe that's the most important portrait of Jesus in the book of Revelation—the portrait of One who can be trusted. One who will see me through.

I'm like a child who cuddles up with Mommy and Daddy in their big bed when the thunder and lightning outside my window frighten me. Being in their bed doesn't make the thunder any less loud or the lightning any less frightening. The wind doesn't stop blowing; the rain doesn't stop falling. But being in my parents' bed puts my mind at ease. Mom and Dad love me. They will protect me. And that is how I can sleep at night, even in the midst of a storm.

Revelation depicts storms blowing all around us. Those winds have raged against the earth ever since Adam ate of the tree of knowledge of good and evil, and they will continue to rage until Jesus returns. Our lives may be interrupted and inconvenienced by the storms; the storms may cause pain and death. But somehow, knowing that we are safe in the loving arms of Christ makes it all better. As long as He is with us and as long as He promises that in the end we will be with Him in heaven, we can endure any storm.

The key to Revelation is to focus on Jesus, the One who loves you—the One who gives you hope, who meets your needs, who is worthy, who assures victory, who controls all things, who dries your tears, who defends you, who planned your salvation, who rescues you, who forgives you, who avenges you, who is your Bridegroom, who prepares a home for you, and who is coming for you. In short, Jesus is the One who helps you sleep at night. That's the Jesus of Revelation.

It's getting late. It is time for me to go to bed, but before I turn out the light I'll take another look at the Jesus I find in Revelation. That's the best way I know to have sweet dreams. Jesus is the One who helps me sleep at night.

Good night, and I hope I see you in the morning—the resurrection morning, that is, when the Jesus we have met here in the book of Revelation comes to awaken us to an eternal day.

If you have been blessed by reading this book, you will also want to read these:

Conversations With Jesus

Jerry D. Thomas

What you wish you could say.

What you long to hear.

What would it be like to have a conversation with Jesus? What would a few uninterrupted moments of "face time" with the Savior mean to you? When you were hurting? When you had doubts? When you were angry, afraid, or grief-stricken?

What would you say to Him? What might He say to You?

During His time on this earth, Jesus had many conversations with ordinary people who struggled with many of the same issues we do today. Listen in on some of these conversations recorded in the Bible. You'll discover that just as He spoke to Mary, or Peter, He will speak to you.

Paperback, 128 pages.   ISBN 10: 0-8163-2088-8

The TEAM

Kim Allan Johnson

From eternity the Father, Son, and Holy Spirit have been One.

Jesus prayed that the church would be one. For more than 2,000 years, Satan has worked to defeat Jesus' aim. Kim Allan Johnson, author of *The Gift* and *The Morning,* shares in this book his conviction that God is calling the Seventh-day Adventist Church to portray the union of the Trinity.

It's time for the church to reflect more than the culture in which it exists. By the Holy Spirit, it can reflect something of the glory of God. As a part of the church, you can become an ambassador of reconciliation and relational healing.

Paperback, 176 pages.   ISBN 10: 0-8163-2203-1

Order from your ABC by calling **1-800-765-6955**, or get online and shop our virtual store at **http//www.AdventistBookCenter.com.**
- Read a chapter from your favorite book
- Order online
- Sign up for e-mail notices on new products